By the same author

Paris: A Literary Companion

A Literary Companion
to Venice

Ian Littlewood

St. Martin's Griffin
New York

Library of Congress Cataloging-in-Publication Data

Littlewood, Ian.
A literary companion to Venice / Ian Littlewood.
p.   cm.
"A Thomas Dunne book."
Enl. ed. of: Venice. 1991.
Includes bibliographical references and index.
ISBN 0-312-13113-5 (pbk.)
1. Venice (Italy)—Tours.   2. Literary landmarks—Italy—
Venice—Guidebooks.   3. Venice (Italy)—Literary
collections.   I. Littlewood, Ian. Venice.   II. Title.
DG672.L54   1995
914.5'3104929—dc20   95-5220   CIP

First published in Great Britain by John Murray

First St. Martin's Griffin Edition: June 1995
10 9 8 7 6 5 4 3 2 1

For Ayumi

CONTENTS

ILLUSTRATIONS

(between pages 148 and 149)

The author and publishers wish to thank the following for permission to reproduce the illustrations: Ancient Art and Architecture Collection, No. 3; Osvaldo Böhm, Venice, Nos. 17, 18; Bridgeman Art Library, No. 1; Mary Evans Picture Library, Nos. 5, 13, 14; Explorer, Paris, No. 6; *Illustrated London News*, No. 16; Mansell Collection, No. 12; National Gallery, No. 11; Scala, Nos. 2, 4; Scala and Ca' Rezzonico, No. 10; Scala and Biblioteca Querini Stampalia, No. 7; Duke of Bedford's Collection, Woburn Abbey, No. 8.

PREFACE

'Abhorrent, green, slippery city,' D. H. Lawrence called it. Venice has never been loved by those who want to change the world. Prophets, moralists, people with missions and ambitions, tend to be impatient of its endless windings and quietly reflective surfaces. Its obsession with the past offends their sense of purpose. At once shabby and narcissistic, it attracts admirers of a different kind. 'The deposed, the defeated, the disenchanted, the wounded, or even only the bored,' observed Henry James, 'have seemed to find there something that no other place could give.'

Writers, many of them, they have served Venice well, and she has returned the compliment by remaining much as they described her. Plenty of cities have been preserved for us in literature; the eerie charm of Venice is that it has also, to a large extent, been preserved in reality. If James could again settle into his gondola, he would have no trouble in finding the polished steps of 'a little empty *campo* . . . with an old well in the middle, an old church on one side and tall Venetian windows looking down.' The shadowy buildings whose outlines were known to the young Casanova still rise around us as we walk by night through the Campo Sant'Angelo. Thomas Coryate, standing once more on the Rialto bridge, would recognize quite enough to bring back memories of his stay in 1608. Even a pilgrim like Felix Fabri would be able to renew acquaintance with churches he visited on his way to the Holy Land at the end of the fifteenth century.

For us, on the edge of a different millennium, it is still possible to sit outside a café in Venice, read their words, look up and nod in recognition. In this extravagant theatre we can with equal ease find settings for the murder of a Renaissance prince or the seduction of an eighteenth-century nun, the execution of a dissolute friar or the melancholy thoughts of a Victorian poet.

The range of material is vast. 'A man to visit Italy and not to write a book about it,' remarked Landor. 'Was ever such a thing heard of?' Not often, it seems. Readers will no doubt be dismayed by many omissions. Detailed accounts of processions, festivals and ceremonies have been kept to a minimum, as have descriptions of buildings. I have usually preferred byways to highways: there will be no tour of the Doge's Palace, no guide to the mosaics of St Mark's, no helpful words on the paintings in the Frari.

This is a guide-book, but it is only in part about the familiar city of churches, palaces and canals. From certain kinds of writing, often by the sort of people James had in mind, another Venice emerges – elusive, unwholesome, perhaps a little unsafe. This other Venice owes more to myth than to brick and stone. Tainted with past iniquity, sluttish under her regal garb, she invites a kind of surrender that can tempt even the most respectable. Today we scarcely notice, for the place is ill-adapted to the urgency of modern tourism; its first requirement is time. Only to those who linger here after they have seen the sights, knowing that they should have left, does it reveal itself. In putting the book together, I have tried to recover something of this ambiguous appeal.

The chapters are arranged in the form of six walks which will take the determined reader into every part of the city. The final chapter touches on a few of the neighbouring islands. For those who would like to follow the suggested routes, maps are provided. Alternatively, and delightfully, one can trust to luck. Anyone who stays in Venice long enough or goes back often enough will sooner or later stumble upon everything mentioned in these pages.

1

DORSODURO

SANTA MARIA DELLA SALUTE

To enter Venice by train, claimed Thomas Mann, is like entering a palace by the back door. We shall enter by the front, San Giorgio on our left, the Doge's Palace on our right, as we sweep towards the mouth of the Grand Canal. Before us, a sight that Coryate and Evelyn never saw: rising behind the customs house at the eastern tip of Dorsoduro are the stately domes of Santa Maria della Salute.

In the autumn of 1630 the plague receded, leaving almost a third of the city's population dead. Among the survivors it was an occasion for gratitude. The Republic commissioned Baldassare Longhena to build a church in honour of the Virgin. It was to be 'strange, worthy and beautiful,' the architect declared, a building 'in the shape of a round "machine", such as had never been seen, or invented either in its whole or in part from any other church in the city.'[1] In retrospect, Longhena's optimism seems wholly justified. His

design is an astonishing success. With its majestic cupolas and
baroque façade, the Salute has become so much a part of our
image of Venice that its absence from early illustrations leaves
us with a sense of something incomplete.

At the entrance of the city the church greets us, according to
Henry James, 'like some great lady on the threshold of her
saloon':

> She is more ample and serene, more seated at her door,
> than all the copyists have told us, with her domes and
> scrolls, her scolloped buttresses and statues forming a
> pompous crown, and her wide steps disposed on the
> ground like the train of a robe.[2]

Prominent among the statues, above the architrave of the
left-hand chapel, is a figure that caught the eye of the French
poet Théophile Gautier. He had arrived in Venice in the
summer of 1850 on a rainy night which allowed him to
glimpse only a tantalizing shadow of the city around him. In
the morning he ran to his balcony in the Hotel Europa and
looked out across the Grand Canal towards the Salute. There
'a figure of Eve in the most gallant state of undress smiled at us
from a cornice under a shaft of sunlight'.[3]

The interior of the church is dominated, as the terms of
Longhena's commission stipulated that it should be, by the
high altar. Horatio Brown, an Englishman who lived in
Venice from 1879 and was one of its most tireless chroniclers,
describes the scene at the annual festival of the Salute on 21
November, commemorating the city's salvation from the
plague:

> Inside the church, the devout light the candles they have
> carried, one taking the fire from another, and press
> forward after the priests up to the altar rails; there the
> tapers are handed over to the sacristans and placed beside
> the high altar, where Madonna stands, triumphing over a
> figure of the plague. Thousands and thousands of candles
> are passed over the rails until the whole space by the altar
> seems like one solid wall of embossed gold as the flames
> waver and flicker in the draught. In return for their

candles and some centesimi, the pious receive a picture of Madonna, which is devoutly kissed and put away inside their shirts or shawls . . . [4]

And when the religious business is done, the *festa* moves on to the neighbouring wine-shops and eating-houses.

These occasions must have had their drawbacks for the church authorities. Henri de Régnier observed with pleasure a restrained notice in the Salute at the turn of the century: 'Out of respect for God and Saint Mary, you are requested not to spit on the ground, but to use, for preference, your handkerchief.'

At night the area round the Salute has a charm increased by its silence. John Addington Symonds, the author of *Renaissance in Italy*, was a friend of Horatio Brown and another Englishman who found in Venice a congenial release from the rigidities of late Victorian England. A long love affair with his gondolier, Angelo Fusato, tied him to Venice through the 1880s until his death in 1893, and for part of each year he rented a small flat attached to Brown's house on the Zattere. In one of the essays in *A Venetian Medley* he describes a night-time stroll towards the Punta della Dogana:

Tonight . . . the waning moon will rise late through veils of *scirocco*. Over the bridges of San Cristoforo and San Gregorio, through the deserted Calle di Mezzo, my friend and I walk in darkness, pass the marble basements of the Salute, and push our way along its Riva to the point of the Dogana. We are out at sea alone, between the Canalazzo and the Giudecca. A moist wind ruffles the water and cools our forehead. It is so dark that we can only see San Giorgio by the light reflected on it from the Piazzetta. The same light climbs the Campanile of S. Mark, and shows the golden angel in a mystery of gloom. The only noise that reaches us is a confused hum from the Piazza. Sitting and musing there, the blackness of the water whispers in our ears a tale of death. And now we hear a plash of oars, and gliding through the darkness comes a single boat. One man leaps upon the landing-place without a word and disappears. There is another wrapped in a military cloak asleep. I see his face beneath me, pale and quiet. The *barcaruolo* turns the point in silence. From the darkness they came; into the darkness they have gone.[5]

CAMPIELLO BARBARO

From the Salute we can walk past the church and campo of San Gregorio and then on to the Ponte San Gregorio mentioned by Symonds. A short way beyond the bridge, ivy spills over the walls of the ancient Palazzo Dario, where Henri de Régnier lived in 1899 and 1901. In the beautiful little Campiello Barbaro, with its picture shops and its three gaunt trees, there is a plaque to his memory on the wall beside the curving bridge. Behind are the dark red walls of the palace. The inscription tells us that he wrote '*venezianamente*', 'Venetianly'. It is an apt expression. Certainly his novel *L'Altana* and the *Esquisses vénitiennes* are penetrated by the atmosphere of the place:

> As I write these words, the evening light thickens over the Grand Canal, the bells sound under a grey November sky. From my table by the window I see the gondolas glide over the water with their black Harlequins at the stern. Here and there a light goes up in the façade of a palace.[6]

Another time he will look out at the silent waters of the little canal that runs alongside the Campiello Barbaro and note the gondolas, stripped of their cushions and *felzi*, waiting idly for the spring to come again. Venice in general and the Palazzo Dario in particular offered a perfect context for the seductive mixture of melancholy and nostalgia which was his characteristic vein. When he catches sight through his window of a group of strangers, Baedekers in hand, asking directions of a policeman, he merely hopes that they won't seek out, through this tangle of streets, the traghetto San Gregorio; for it is here, 'in this district so melancholy and so solitary . . . that the house stands in which I live – happier than a Doge.'[7]

An earlier inhabitant of the Palazzo Dario, from 1838–1842,

was Ruskin's friend Rawdon Brown, a later one, in the 1970s, Kit Lambert, manager of the rock group The Who. Between the scrupulous antiquarian and the flamboyant, dope-ravaged Lambert there could scarcely have been a wider gap. But they were both lonely men to whom happiness did not come easily, and both of them were happy in Venice. While Florence was a natural resort in the nineteenth century for exiled couples, Venice became increasingly the haven of individuals. A string of writers and artists from the late nineteenth century onwards – men as different as Symonds, Brown, James, Proust, Corvo – seemed to find in its passivity and its decadence and its ambiguous femininity an atmosphere that allowed them to breathe more freely. Often, in spite of their sociability, they were solitary figures, often homosexual. Whereas other writers passed through Venice and admired what is to be admired, these were caught in her toils. And they wrote of the city with corresponding intensity – about the beauties she displays, but more particularly about the less familiar beauties that she half-conceals.

Rawdon Brown had come here in the summer of 1833 to look for the burial place of Thomas Mowbray (see p. 114), and for the next fifty years, until his death, he stayed:

> I scarcely wake in the morning but I thank God that he has let me spend my days in Venice; and sometimes of an evening, when I go to the Piazzetta, I am afraid to shut my eyes, lest when I open them I should find it had all been a dream.[8]

In the 'Sonnet to Rawdon Brown' Browning pictures him about to return to England for a last sight of it before he dies. On the point of leaving, he looks back at Venice: 'What a sky, / A sea, this morning! One last look! Good-by, / Cà Pesaro . . .' He never leaves.

RIO DI SAN VIO

This eastern spur of Dorsoduro has a distinctive tone which is reflected in the absence of large hotels and the sprinkling of smaller, more discreet *pensioni*.[9] It has long been associated with foreign visitors, but not, for the most part, with those who travel on expense accounts or in troublesome groups. If E. M. Forster had set a novel in Venice, this would surely have been the place for his more sympathetic characters. The atmosphere of its quiet streets readily suggests the image of English visitors of a certain age, cultured and unassuming, setting off from rather spartan rooms for a serious morning's sight-seeing. Perhaps they would not themselves patronize the Anglican church of St George on the corner of the Campo San Vio and the Calle della Chiesa, but its presence in the area would seem a fitting legacy from a slightly earlier age.

The Campo San Vio is separated from the Palazzo Loredan and the recently established Cini collection[10] by the Rio di San Vio, a canal that is usually busy with barges transporting anything from eighteenth-century furniture to crates of coca-cola. It was here that Baron Corvo suffered the indignity described in 'On Cascading into the Canal'. Corvo, whose real name was Frederick Rolfe, had arrived in Venice in the summer of 1908. He was forty-eight years old and had so far enjoyed a life of almost unrelieved failure. He had failed to become a Roman Catholic priest, he had failed as a painter, and his careers as schoolmaster and photographer had been equally unremarkable. He was, however, the author of a brilliant, patchy work of fiction, *Hadrian the Seventh*. It was his literary talent, combined with a prickly sort of charm, that enabled him to find a series of patrons with whom he inevitably quarrelled. The most recent of these was the archaeologist Richard Dawkins, who had brought him to Venice. A decent man some ten years younger than Rolfe, Dawkins had private means and shared, from a timid distance, his companion's interest in the homosexual possibilities of a city full of gondoliers. They took rooms on the fourth floor of the Hotel Belle Vue et de Russie, at the corner of St Mark's Square, intending to settle down for a six-week holiday.

Rolfe believed that it was the part of a gentleman to spend lavishly, and his belief was if anything reinforced by the fact that it was Dawkins's money that he was spending. Within a month the two had parted company and Rolfe was on his own in Venice. Until his death in 1913 he was frequently advised, cajoled, and bribed to leave by other members of the English colony, but the place had taken possession of him. With an enormous Waterman fountain pen and a padlocked laundry basket which contained the rest of his possessions, he moved about Venice for the next five years, running up debts, feuding with the resident English, chasing gondoliers, and writing with lyrical passion about the city he had adopted.

Corvo's main enthusiasm was for the various craft that plied the narrow Venetian canals, and he himself became an accomplished oarsman. Late one cheerless autumn afternoon he had set off from the Bucintoro club with his gondolier, Emilio Sacripan – 'Emily'. The man was in disgrace at the time, Corvo explains, and had been threatened with dismissal:

So he was on his best behaviour when we set forth that dull cold afternoon on the top of a high tide and a flowing sea, from the Club, up Canal Grande past La Salute, turning off at the Duchess of Madrid's red and yellow posted palace with the gilded Florentine lilies, to go up Rio di San Vio. And then, just after you pass the Erastian temple, the Rio di San Vio narrows, and is crossed by a bridge, before it widens again into a very decent canal with quays for pedestrians on both sides of it. We had swirled through the narrow part and under the bridge, when the calamity occurred. I was rowing at the prow, and Emily was steering at the poop, the pace being my usual swift and hectic one. A big unwieldy barea of firewood came suddenly towards us, rowed by two of my former gondoglieri, Piero Venerand and Ermengildo Vianel, who had gotten a better winter job than mine in the firewood business of the latter's father. To avoid collision Emily precipitately twitched my *barcheta* to one side without much judgement. I incontinently lost my balance; and, disliking the notion of crashing ignominiously inboard to sprawl among oars and *forcole*, I made no ado whatever, but just gripped my short pipe more tightly between my teeth, and took a neat header into the canal, passing right under the approaching wood barge.

As I shot through the air I saw all the hands of all the
people on the two *fondamente* being flung to heaven, and I
heard all their voices bawling, 'Ara, Ara! O Mariaver-
gine! For pleasure here is an English going to drown
himself fastidiously!' So as soon as I got under water, I
told myself that the said English had better give these
people something truly rare and wholesome to cough
about. Wherefore I swam, submerged, about thirty yards
up the Rio, passionlessly emerging (to a fanfare of yells) in
a totally unexpected place, with a perfectly stony face,
and the short pipe still stiff and rigid in an immovable
mouth.[11]

The Accademia

A hundred yards beyond Corvo's canal the calle runs up to the
side-wall of the Accademia. The most entertaining travellers
are rarely the best art critics. Dutiful comments prompted by a
morning in a famous gallery make dull reading, as countless
volumes of eighteenth- and nineteenth-century memoirs tes-
tify. Only occasionally do the paintings meet their match.
W. D. Howells describes a Victorian paterfamilias contem-
plating Titian's *John the Baptist* in Room 6, with his family in
respectful attendance. After a few moments, his verdict is
reached: '"Quite my idea of the party's character," he said;
and then silently and awfully led his domestic train away.'[12]

Théophile Gautier was one traveller who could bring an
element of poetry to his description of the paintings in the
Accademia. He was moved, in particular, by Titian's great
Pietà – 'this grave and melancholy canvas, whose subject
seems almost a foreboding':

> In truth, Titian never painted a body more lifeless. Under
> this green skin, in these bluish veins, there remains no
> drop of blood, the crimson pulse of life has stopped for
> ever. . . . For the first time the great Venetian has been
> abandoned by his old, unalterable serenity. The shadow
> of approaching death seems to struggle with the sunlight
> that was always on the painter's palette, and to envelop

the canvas in a crepuscular chill. The hand of the artist went cold before completing its task, as witnessed by the inscription in black letters traced at the corner of the painting: *Quod Tizianus inchoatum reliquit Palma reverenter absolvit Deoque dicavit opus.* 'The work which Titian left unfinished, Palma reverently completed and offered to God.'[13]

Of the anecdotes that have attached themselves to various pictures, one of the most revealing concerns Veronese's encounter with the Inquisition over the painting, then called *The Last Supper*, which he had executed for the refectory of SS. Giovanni e Paolo. What troubled the somewhat humourless Inquisitors was that Veronese seemed to have been more interested in the decorative and artistic possibilities of the scene than in its religious content. He was called to account on 8 July 1573:

Question. What is the meaning of those men dressed in the German fashion each with a halberd in his hand? . . .
Answer. We painters take the same licence that is permitted to poets and jesters. I have placed these two halberdiers – the one eating, the other drinking – by the staircase, to be supposed ready to perform any duty that may be required of them; it appearing to me quite fitting that the master of such a house, who was rich and great (as I have been told), should have such attendants.
Q. That fellow dressed like a buffoon, with the parrot on his wrist – for what purpose is *he* introduced into the canvas?
A. For ornament, as is usually done.[14]

And so it goes on. 'Were you commissioned by any person to paint Germans and buffoons, and such-like things in this picture?' 'No, my lord.' 'Does it appear to you fitting that at our Lord's last supper you should paint buffoons, drunkards, Germans, dwarfs, and similar indecencies?' 'No, my lord,' Veronese again answers prudently.

This was clearly not a meeting of minds. Veronese's freewheeling notions of subject-matter belonged to a more expansive age, when the Renaissance was in full flower. It was his good fortune that the Counter-Reformation had been taken up with only moderate zeal by the Venetians. The Inquisitors initially wanted the offending items repainted, but a happier solution was found by simply retitling the picture. As *The Supper in the House of Levi* it could comfortably accommodate dwarfs, parrots, buffoons, and even heretical Germans.

Attempts to improve the reader's acquaintance with paintings not present to the eye are a hazardous business for the casual traveller. In *The Annunciation* by a follower of Veronese, E. V. Lucas helpfully informs us that 'we find a good vivid angel, but she has a terrific leg.'[15] Perhaps, on the whole, it is better to take the line of the admirable Dr John Moore, father of the hero of Corunna. Writing of his visit to Italy in 1776 he eschews the usual banalities of connoisseurship and offers instead a cautionary tale. Some years earlier, he tells us, he had been going round a gallery with a group of five or six other Englishmen, among them a gentleman who affected an enthusiastic passion for the fine arts:

> From the moment we entered the rooms he began to display all the refinements of his taste; he instructed us what to admire, and drew us away with every sign of disgust when we stopped a moment at an uncelebrated picture. We were afraid of appearing pleased with any thing we saw, till he informed us whether or not it was worth looking at. He shook his head at some, tossed up his nose at others; commended a few, and pronounced sentence on every piece as he passed along, with the most imposing tone of sagacity. . . .
>
> We at length came to the St John, by Raphael, and here this man of taste stopped short in an extasy of admiration – One of the company had already passed it, without minding it, and was looking at another picture; on which the connoisseur bawled out – 'Good God, Sir! what are you about?' The honest gentleman started, and stared around to know what crime he had been guilty of.
>
> 'Have you eyes in your head, Sir?' continued the connoisseur: 'Don't you know St John when you see him?'

'St. John!' replied the other, in amazement. 'Aye, Sir, St. John the Baptist, *in propria persona*.'

'I don't know what you mean, Sir,' said the gentleman, peevishly.

'Don't you?' rejoined the connoisseur; 'then I'll endeavour to explain myself. I mean St. John in the wilderness, by the divine Raffaelle Sanzio da Urbino, and there he stands by your side. – Pray, my dear Sir, will you be so obliging as to bestow a little of your attention on that foot? Does it not start from the wall? Is it not perfectly out of the frame? Did you ever see such colouring? They talk of Titian; can Titian's colouring excel that? What truth, what nature in the head! To the elegance of the antique, here is joined the simplicity of nature.'

We stood listening in silent admiration, and began to imagine we perceived all the perfections he ennumerated; when a person in the Duke of Orleans' service came and informed us that the original, which he presumed was the picture we wished to see, was in another room; the Duke having allowed a painter to copy it. *That* which we had been looking at was a very wretched daubing, done from the original by some obscure painter, and had been thrown, with other rubbish, into a corner; where the Swiss had accidentally discovered it, and had hung it up merely by way of covering up the vacant space on the wall, till the other should be replaced.[16]

ZATTERE

'And on the Zattere,' wrote Horatio Brown, 'the air is laden with the perfume of honeysuckle and other creepers that trail over the wall of Princess Dolgorouki's garden.'[17] To reach this beautiful fondamenta we can walk up the broad, leafy Rio Terrà M. Foscarini – Rio Terrà indicating that it was once a canal – which runs alongside the Accademia and opens on to the Zattere just beside the church of the Gesuati. Brown's own house, with a relief of St George and Dragon above the door, was nearby at no. 560. He was one of several resident and

visiting Englishmen who favoured this area towards the end of
the nineteenth century. In his later years Ruskin too stayed on
the Zattere, and Count Zorzi recalls coming upon him chop-
ping wood in the courtyard of what is now the Pensione
Calcina. For the diligent expatriate, *Murray's Handbook* for
1877 notes that Italian lessons can be had from Signora Michiel
at 420, Zattere gli Incurabili, close to where Brown was
living.

The Incurabili of this address is the massive building for
delinquent youth a short way along the Zattere towards the
Salute. It was established in 1522 in response to the spread of
syphilis, which had first appeared in Venice some thirty years
earlier – the Gallic disease, as it was firmly called. (This was
not merely an Italian quirk. Syphilis, like the Devil, always
comes from outside – practically every country in Europe
shuffled the responsibility on to one of its neighbours and
named the disease accordingly.) On 22 February 1522 a pro-
clamation was addressed to the increasing numbers afflicted by
the French pox, 'some of whom in their impotence loiter on
the streets and in the passageways of churches and public
buildings both at Rialto and at San Marco to beg for their
living'. They were ordered to repair to the hospital without
delay.

Among the first to work here were members of the newly
founded Society of Jesus. Along with Loyola himself, they
spent the spring and summer of 1537 in Venice waiting for
papal permission to make a pilgrimage to the Holy Land.
Forty years later the Portuguese Simon Rodriguez, who had
been one of their number, set down an account of these
months. At a time when syphilis and leprosy were popularly
thought to be transmissible merely by the infected breath of
the sufferer,[18] it must have required strong convictions to turn
to this sort of work with any enthusiasm. To overcome their
repugnance, it was not enough for these early Jesuits to
undertake the routine business of caring for the sick:

> In the hospital of The Incurabili, a leper, or one suffering
> from a form of skin disease, covered all over by a kind of
> pestilential mange, called one of the fathers and asked him

to scratch his back. The father diligently performed this service, but whilst he was doing so he was suddenly struck with horror and nausea, and with the terror of contracting the contagious disease. But since he wanted to master himself and to suppress his own rebellious spirit rather than take thought for the future, he put into his mouth a finger covered with pus and sucked it. . . . For this father, who had done the act in good faith and fervour in order to conquer himself, the words of our Lord Jesus Christ were fulfilled: 'And if they drink any deadly thing, it shall not hurt them.'[19]

This was excellent in its way, but the Venetians were never quite comfortable with religious fervour. For most of the city's history the Jesuits were kept at a cautious distance.

More congenial, at least according to Corvo, was the ancient order of the Poveri Gesuati, founded in the late fourteenth century and suppressed in 1668. Their church, which was built after the order had been taken over by the Dominicans, is one of the landmarks passed by Corvo's hero, Nicholas Crabbe, as he wanders through the city. Like Corvo himself, he is obliged by poverty to spend long nights sleeping in his *sandolo* on the lagoon or tramping the streets:

The whole quay of the Zattere extended itself before him. He set himself to pace it from end to end. The drizzle ceased, and a warm haze bloomed on the darkness. He kept moving, to dry his drenched clothes.

Midnight sounded, and the stroke of one. The last ferries left the pontoons by the church of the Gesuati. He thought it a pity that that order of Gesuati, which is three centuries older than the Gesuiti, should have become extinct. The Jesuats always had a most respectable reputation . . .

On the distant bank of the wide canal of Zuecca, the lengthy line of lights along Spinalonga fluttered like little pale daffodils in a night-mist coloured like the bloom on the fruit of the vine. Great quiet reigned. He prayed, to comfort the minutes as they fled by. Holy thoughts were his, and ardent yearnings, in his unhoused loneliness . . .[20]

On his way from the church of the Gesuati to the tip of the Zattere Nicholas Crabbe would have passed not only the Incurabili but also the imposing wall of the old salt warehouse just beyond. Not a sight much regarded by tourists, it was singled out by the art critic Adrian Stokes in his discussion of the beauty of Venetian brick. One thinks of Venice as a city of stone, he remarks, 'because stone is the final material, the head and the fruit of walls of brick and stucco. Emergent from duller surfaces, the white stone glows. Istrian stone is nearly always the boundary as well as the relevant mark upon the wall.'[21] But the unhidden brick in Venice has an attraction of its own:

> Some of the early Gothic and Renaissance Gothic palaces from which the stucco has peeled are remarkably charming. Such rosy brick, like the occasional greenness of enclosed gardens that appears over walls, or like huge Venetian red sails and blinds, suggests an islanded peace, an earth substance matured by the sun, an aged country warmth. Another instance is the Abbazia San Gregorio on the Grand Canal or the huge wall of the salt warehouse on the Zattere, the warmest pitch in Venice on many days of winter.[22]

SAN TROVASO

The Rio di San Trovaso is one of the main highways between the Giudecca Canal and the Grand Canal. If we turn off the Zattere and walk beside it along the Fondamenta Nani, we can see across the canal, just before the church of San Trovaso, a relic of earlier times. On the corner of the Rio dei Ognissanti, sloping into the water, is a ramp usually occupied by half a dozen gondolas, hulls to the air, waiting to be planed and painted. Behind them is the open workshop where they are built and overhauled. At the end of the sixteenth century there were ten thousand gondolas in Venice, today a few hundred at most. Even this boatyard of San Trovaso survives partly by subsidy from an international committee.

There are shelf-loads of books – histories, anthologies, picture books, academic studies – devoted solely to the gondola. We do not have to read far to stumble on at least one explanation for this: it is the gondola which focuses most sharply the intriguing association between Venice and death. The sumptuary laws which stripped the gondola of colour and left it bare of all but the most austere form of decoration were in the end responsible for its enduring hold on our imagination. The Romantics were quick to respond: 'Just like a coffin clapt in a canoe,' wrote Byron. And Shelley, 'I can only compare them to moths of which a coffin might have been the crysalis.' Arriving in Venice for the first time James Fenimore Cooper notes their 'solemn and hearse-like look'. Twenty years later, Wagner, already fearful of cholera, had to force himself to get into one, so disagreeably did it suggest the idea of taking part in a funeral procession. 'Black as nothing else on earth except a coffin' is Gustave von Aschenbach's prophetic thought in Thomas Mann's novella.

Venice is traditionally a city of pleasure and fantasy; but an equally powerful tradition links it with images of what is sinister – with pestilence and decay, the assassin's hand and the secret ways of Venetian justice. There is always the sense both of the carnival and the dungeon, the mask and what the mask conceals, of a city that is, in Mann's words, 'half fairy-tale, half snare'. And as Mann realized, it is the peculiar fascination of the gondola that it enshrines both these elements. The point had already been made in characteristic fashion by Henry James:

> The little closed cabin of this perfect vehicle, the movement, the darkness and the plash, the indistinguishable swerves and twists, all the things you don't see and all the things you do feel – each dim recognition and obscure arrest is a possible throb of your sense of being floated to your doom, even when the truth is simply and sociably that you are going out to tea. Nowhere else is anything as

innocent so mysterious, nor anything as mysterious so
pleasantly deterrent to protest.[23]

As so often, James's imagery brushes the dangerous edge of
the sexual before declaring itself respectably social. More
lightly, less respectably, Byron had put the same perception
into verse:

> And up and down the long canals they go,
>   And under the Rialto shoot along,
> By night and day, all paces, swift or slow,
>   And round the theatres, a sable throng,
> They wait in their dusk livery of woe, –
>   But not to them do woeful things belong,
> For sometimes they contain a deal of fun,
>   Like mourning coaches when the funeral's done.[24]

It is hard to feel anything but regret for the passing of such a
graceful and romantic vehicle as the gondola. The one positive
consequence was perhaps that it forced lethargic tourists to
their feet. In former times walking had been firmly discour-
aged. It was the sort of thing that a few dubious expatriates
might get up to, but not the readers of *Cook's Handbook* for
1875:

> A long residence is necessary to enable any one to find his
> way through the labyrinthine streets. Besides which,
> nobody ever thinks of walking in Venice. It is poor policy
> to do so. Gondolas are very cheap, and very comfortable.
> Museums, churches, and picture galleries are very tiring.
> And much valuable time is lost in wandering north,
> south, and east, in order to find a place in the west.[25]

As the gondolas and boatyards have disappeared, so ro-
mance has accrued to the survivors – which receive cor-
respondingly more attention from writers, painters, and
photographers. The *squero* opposite the Fondamenta Nani
already had an honourable tradition. It was here that Nicholas
Crabbe rented lodgings for the beautiful and ambiguous Zildo
in *The Desire and Pursuit of the Whole*, securing a room 'which
gave a view of the rio in front flanked by the lovely old squero

with the trees and green and church, and the Rio di Ognisanti
with the Long Bridge and the Zuecca canal, to right, and left,
respectively.'[26]

Just a year before Crabbe, the slightly less fictional figure of
Ezra Pound had turned up in the same place. He had arrived in
Venice in the spring of 1908, twenty-two years old with a
broken engagement and an abortive academic career behind
him, and dreams of literary fame ahead. At first, he took a
room a short distance away near the Ponte San Vio 'by the
soap-smooth stone posts where San Vio/meets with il Canal
Grande'. At the end of June he moved from there to lodgings
on the corner of the Fondamenta Nani and the Calle dei Frati,
overlooking the *squero*, which he blithely claimed to be 'probably an exact replica of what it was in the sixth century'. It was
while he was living here that his first volume of poems, *A
Lume Spento*, was privately printed in Venice. The city, and
particularly this part of it, became for him, as it has for others,
a focus of nostalgia and a source of images of past happiness. In
a darker future these lines were written for the *Pisan Cantos* but
later omitted:

> San Giorgio, San Trovaso . . .
> Will I ever see the Giudecca again?
>   or the lights against it or Ca Foscari?
>   or Ca Giustinian . . .
>   or the boats moored off le Zattere . . .

Perhaps no city but Venice lends itself so powerfully to
nostalgia because no other city resists time so faithfully or
marks its passage so clearly. Everywhere one turns, the stones
of Venice record the wearing, transforming effects of successive centuries; and yet the stones themselves have survived.
Released in 1958 from the madhouse where his sympathies
with Italian fascism had landed him after the war, Pound
returned to this part of Venice a few years later to spend much
of his last decade living in the nearby Calle Querini. As he
walked through the Piazzetta in sad old age and saw the
unfettered young of the late sixties sprawled on the steps of the
column where St Theodore stands with his crocodile, he must
have thought back to the months he had spent in Venice sixty

years earlier, when his life seemed able to take whatever
direction he chose:

> And
> I came here in my young youth
>   and lay there under the crocodile
> By the column, looking East on Friday,
> And I said: Tomorrow I will lie on the South side
> And the day after, south west.
> And at night they sang in the gondolas
> And in the barche with lanthorns;
> The prows rose silver on silver
>   taking light in the darkness.[27]

No other place can hold one's youth in amber quite so
perfectly.

SOTTOPORTICO DEL CASIN

Just before the end of the Rio San Trovaso a left turn across the
bridge and into the Calle della Toletta will take us towards the
Campo San Barnaba, which we enter through the Sottoportico del Casin. Surmounted by handsome old chimney-
pots, this passageway takes its name from the *casino* that was
once situated here. When public gambling halls were closed in
1774, the business simply went private, and the spread of
casinos was the immediate result. They could be used as places
of rendezvous when occasion offered, but their main function
is indicated by Mutinelli's thundering denunciation in his
Annali Urbani:

> This was where, amid gossiping, gaming and sneering,
> debauchery called itself gallantry, impudence urbanity,
> and vice pleasure; where the lustful behaviour of the
> women was brought to new heights by the rivalry of
> others who sought to replace them; where, almost to a
> man, the winners laughed in the face of the losers; where
> the losers yelled in vexation at every card, some blaming
> themselves, others someone else, and so loudly and with

such violence that they were sometimes on the edge of coming to blows.[28]

PONTE DEI PUGNI

If we bear left across the Campo San Barnaba, we shall come almost at once to a small bridge with a barge of brightly coloured fruit moored beside it. This is the most famous of the city's Ponti dei Pugni. The opposing pairs of footprints set into the top of the bridge mark the place where battles once took place between the ancient factions of the Castellani and the Nicolotti. The rivalry between these two sections of the Venetian populace dated back to a parish feud in the fourteenth century and was based on a geographical division between the eastern side of the city, which was the territory of the Castellani, and the western, which was inhabited by the Nicolotti. (According to tradition, the two façades of the church of San Trovaso were due to its site on the borderline between the hostile groups; the Castellani could use the south door and the Nicolotti the west.) The enmity between the two factions periodically broke out in street brawls, but for the most part it was channelled into set-piece battles that usually took place in the autumn and early winter, originally with clubs, later with fists. To add to the interest of these occasions, the various bridges were left without parapets, so that the combatants could get drenched as well as bruised.

An abrupt end was put to the tradition of the Guerra dei Pugni at the beginning of the eighteenth century. On 30 September 1705 the combatants on this bridge in San Barnaba progressed from fists to knives and stones. The result was a bloodbath. Thereafter they had to make do with the less dangerous rivalry of the regattas.

CAMPANILE OF THE CARMINI

To the left of the Pontè dei Pugni, rising above the buildings on the other side of the canal, is the campanile of Santa Maria dei Carmini. Before crossing the bridge, we can take a slightly closer look by walking alongside the canal up the pretty Fondamenta Gherardini. From the far end of it we get the best view available of the enclosed campanile. It looks in less than perfect shape today, but it is probably safer than it used to be. Built in the early seventeeth century, the campanile rapidly developed an alarming list. The details of how it was ingeniously straightened by Giuseppe Sardi in 1688 are given in Hugh A. Douglas's excellent guide-book *Venice on Foot*:

> Holes were bored in the brickwork about 70 feet from the ground, on three sides, omitting the side to which it inclined. Into these holes wedges of wood were driven, and then more holes were made and more wood inserted, until there was a complete stratum of wood on these three sides. A strong acid was then applied to the wood, which, being gradually consumed, the whole structure settled down into the vacant space and so resumed its upright position, which it has practically retained ever since. The scars of the operation can be clearly seen in the interior of the building, where there is also a Latin inscription recording the operation.[29]

In his somewhat deadpan manner Captain Douglas, as he then was, goes on to mention the time in 1756 when the campanile was struck by lightning, 'on which occasion the monks, who were ringing the bells, fled in such haste that one of them ran his head against the wall and killed himself'.

CA' REZZONICO

On the far side of the Ponte dei Pugni the fondamenta leads down to the Ca' Rezzonico, described by Henry James as 'thrusting itself upon the water with a peculiar florid assurance, a certain upward toss of its cornice which gives it the air of a rearing sea-horse'.[30] It was in this great seventeenth-century palace that Robert Browning spent his final days. After a long break he had started visiting Venice again in the summer of 1878, usually as the guest of Katharine de Kay

Bronson (see p. 77). Hankering for a palace of his own, he tried to buy the Palazzo Contarini dal Zaffo near the Accademia. The failure of this attempt was a blow to which he was only reconciled some years later when his son Pen, on the strength of a rich American wife, bought the Ca' Rezzonico. Suddenly the feckless Pen, who had otherwise proved rather disappointing, revealed an unsuspected talent. Under his direction the palace was transformed. Again Henry James was on hand to comment, giving the business a malicious gloss in a letter to his sister from the Palazzo Barbaro:

> What Pen has done here, through his American wife's dollars, with the splendid Palazzo Rezzonico, transcends description for the beauty, and, as Ruskin would say, 'wisdom and rightness' of it. It is altogether royal and imperial – but 'Pen' isn't kingly and the *train de vie* remains to be seen. Gondoliers ushering in friends from pensions won't fill it out.[31]

By this time the splendours of the Ca' Rezzonico were no longer of consequence to Browning himself. He had only had six weeks to marvel at his beloved son's achievements. On the evening of 12 December 1889, cheered by news of *Asolando*'s successful publication in England, he died. After lying in state in the ballroom of the palace, his body was transported with due pomp to the chapel of San Michele and thence, two days later, to Westminster Abbey.

Today the palace houses a museum devoted to the attractions of eighteenth-century Venice. Browning's apartment is usually locked, but a plaque beside the land entrance of the palace reminds the visitor of its association with the English poet:

A
ROBERTO BROWNING
MORTO IN QUESTO PALAZZO
IL 12 DICEMBRE 1889
VENEZIA
POSE
'Open my heart and you will see
Graved inside of it, "Italy."'

Palazzi Giustinian

From the upper windows of the Ca' Rezzonico, we can just see
the roofs of the Palazzi Giustinian a few yards further down the
Grand Canal. It was in the middle one of these three palaces
that Wagner completed the second act of *Tristan and Isolde*. He
had arrived in Venice at sunset on 29 August 1858. After a
night at the Danieli he moved into an imposing room here,
overlooking the canal, redecorated it with dramatic red wall-
paper and curtains, and set to work. The daily life he describes
in his autobiography follows a scrupulous routine: work till
two, a meal in St Mark's Square, a walk along the Riva degli
Schiavoni to the Public Gardens, then at nightfall back by
gondola along the darkening canal until he sees the glow of his
lamp, 'the only point of light in the nocturnal façade of the
Palazzo Giustinian'.

Wagner's finances on this first visit were sometimes
stretched. Unable to pay the landlord on one occasion, he
applied for help to Suski, the commissionaire. This enterprising man later appeared with the rent, having borrowed it from
the landlord himself, who was also in business as a money-
lender.

A slightly later resident of the Palazzi Giustinian was W. D.
Howells, who lived for a time in the palace nearest the Salute,
tenant of six huge rooms and a magnificent hall on the *piano
signorile* at a rent of one dollar a day. He had come to Venice in
1861 as American consul – a reward for his flattering bio-
graphy of Lincoln. The job was unclouded by any obligation
to work, and for the next four years he was free to potter about
the city collecting material for a number of books, among
them the amiable reminiscences published in *Venetian Life*
(1866). Much of the average day at the Palazzo Giustinian
seems to have been spent on the balcony, starting with an
agreeable breakfast – 'a cup of coffee, with a little bread and
butter, a musk-melon, and some clusters of white grapes,
more or less':

After our breakfast we began to watch for the gondolas of
the tourists of different nations, whom we came to

distinguish at a glance. Then the boats of the various artisans went by, the carpenter's, the mason's, the plasterer's, with those that sold fuel, and vegetables, and fruit, and fish, to any household that arrested them. From noon till three or four o'clock the Canal was comparatively deserted; but before twilight it was thronged again by people riding out in their open gondolas to take the air after the day's fervour.[32]

One pleasure that Howells enjoyed, denied to most modern visitors, was the view of a Venetian garden at the back of the palace. This was owned by an aged artist who lived on the floor below:

It was full of oleanders and roses, and other bright and odorous blooms, which we could enjoy perfectly well without knowing their names; and I could hardly say whether the garden was more charming when it was in its summer glory, or when, on some rare winter day, a breath from the mountains had clothed its tender boughs and sprays with a light and evanescent flowering of snow. At any season the lofty palace walls rose over it, and shut it in a pensive seclusion which was loved by the old mother of the painter and by his elderly maiden sister. These often walked on its moss-grown paths, silent as the roses and oleanders to which one could have fancied the blossom of their youth had flown; and sometimes there came to them there, grave, black-gowned priests, – for the painter's was a devout family, – and talked with them in tones almost as tranquil as the silence was, save when one of the ecclesiastics placidly took snuff, – it is a dogma of the Church for priests to take snuff in Italy, – and thereafter, upon a prolonged search for his handkerchief, blew a resounding nose.[33]

CALLE DEL MAGAZEN

From the Calle Giustinian, which runs alongside the palace, a series of twisting alleys lead to the Calle del Magazen. The name of the street suggests the working-class associations of the area. The *magazen* was a curiously Italian brand of pawn-shop. For the goods you gave in pawn you would receive two-thirds of their value in money and one-third in cheap wine, allowing you to drink away your family's substance with more than usual convenience. The appearance and atmosphere of these places is described by Casanova in a paragraph of his memoirs which evokes an interesting corner of contemporary working-class life:

> In each of the seventy-two parishes of the city of Venice, there is a big tavern called a *magazzeno*, where wine is sold at retail, which stays open all night, and where one can drink more cheaply than at the other taverns in the city, where food is also provided. One can also eat at the *magazzeno* by sending out for what one wants to the pork butcher's shop, which is also regularly to be found in each parish and which is open all night. The pork butcher also keeps a cook shop, where he prepares execrable food; but since he sells everything cheaply his establishment is of great use to the poor. In the *magazzeno* itself one never sees either members of the nobility or citizens in good circumstances, for cleanliness is not to be found there. These places are frequented only by the common people. They have small rooms containing only a table sur-rounded by benches instead of chairs. [34]

For nineteenth-century tourists, as for their modern counterparts, the ready flow of wine was one of the attractions of European travel. Thomas Cook was himself a teetotaller, and the enthusiasm with which some of his early tourists took to Continental ways plainly distressed him:

> Wine drinking in Italy was then, as it was in France and Switzerland, one of the prevailing torments of the people, though it was thought that the common wines of Italy were less potent than those of France and Switzerland, and I was sometimes grieved to see my parties . . . purchase large quantities of common drinks, the merits of which they were utterly unacquainted with. I had such a

strong feeling in reference to this, and the evils that were already beginning to be manifested in the shape of prevalent diarrhoea amongst some of the weaker of the party, that I remonstrated with them, and said to them on going to the rooms, 'Gentlemen, do not invest your money in diarrhoea.'[35]

To judge from the number of streets which still bear the name Calle del Magazen, this was not a cry that would have touched the Venetians.

AN UNNAMED COURTYARD

The Calle del Magazen opens into the spacious Campo Santa Margherita. On sunny days this is a cheerful spot, animated by market stalls and the usual supply of children. On the far side a series of alleys branch confidently out of the square, all but two of them leading straight into the Canal Santa Margherita. To miss one's way from time to time is inevitable, but these detours are no hardship. A lucky chance might bring you upon the little courtyard which the Irish writer Sean O'Faolain found one day during the hot August weeks of 1948 recorded in *A Summer in Italy*. Venice is prodigal of such unexpected gifts:

I remember one day taking a wrong turning near the Campo Santa Margherita. I should not now be able to find it if my life hung on it. I found myself in a *calle* that ended up in a dead end, a tiny *corte*, and was about to turn back when my eye fell on an old carved block of Verona marble through which a wall has been built in the most cavalier indifference to the craftsman's art. I now know it to be of Verona marble, and an ancient well-head, because I have found out since that, as one might expect, the tireless John [Ruskin] – he who knew all, saw all, told all – also found it in his day, when searching for the land-entrance on the Rio San Pantalon to the house whose Byzantine arches he had spotted from the Ca' Foscari. I cannot believe that one out of ten thousand visitors, or for that matter Venetians, has ever laid eyes on that old Verona well-head.[36]

At its south-western corner the Campo Santa Margherita narrows to a point a few yards from the bare space of the Campo dei Carmini, where tradition once placed the home of Shakespeare's Othello. He was reputed to have lived in the house at the corner of the campo, overlooking the canal. All that remains of the original building is the thoroughly un-Moorish statue, niched in the wall, of an epicene page-boy supporting a shield and looking down the canal. This was confidently identified with Othello himself. 'Indeed,' remarks Howells, 'what can you say to the gondolier, who, in answer to your cavils, points to the knight, with the convincing argument, "There is his statue!"'[37]

SAN NICOLÒ DEI MENDICOLI

A left turn out of the Campo dei Carmini will take us along the fondamenta past the slightly austere cream-coloured façade of Santa Maria del Soccorso at no. 2590. Now an institute for female students at the university, this was earlier the site of a home for fallen women founded at the end of the sixteenth century by the celebrated courtesan Veronica Franco. Even at the time it must have been rare for a courtesan's client to be offered a couple of sonnets in addition to a night of love. Small wonder, perhaps, that Henri III of France carried home a portrait of her in enamel. Later, when poetry and penitence had led her into retirement, she made contact with Montaigne during his visit to Venice in 1580.

Directly in front of Santa Maria del Soccorso we cross over to the fondamenta on the other side of the canal and walk up past the splendid Palazzo Arian, distinguished by its fourteenth-century Gothic windows and the swirl of students who now enliven its courtyard. A short way from here the fondamenta comes to an end beside the ancient campanile of San Nicolò dei Mendicoli, an appealing church restored by the Venice in Peril fund. It was here that the ill-fated hero in the film of Daphne Du Maurier's *Don't Look Now* was working.

The story itself is a modest affair, but out of it Nicholas Roeg created a succession of crisp, lonely images which reflect the atmosphere of Venice in winter with loving delicacy.

In front of the church we can pause in a charming little campo, lapped on both sides by the Rio di San Nicolò. Near the canal is a stone pillar topped by a somewhat weather-beaten lion of St Mark. This reminder of the column in front of the Doge's Palace is not accidental. The flagstaff nearby memorializes, according to the inscription, 'the favours and privileges granted by the Republic to the Nicolotti and their Doge'. What this refers to is the election of a sort of Doge of the Poor, chosen from among the Nicolotti to preside over them and to represent their interests. It was one advantage at least that the Nicolotti could claim over their rivals, the more prosperous Castellani. George Sand records the popular taunt: '*Ti, ti voghi el dose, et mi vogo col dose.*' ('You row for the Doge, but I row with the Doge.')[38]

THE DOCKLANDS

This outer rim of the city, skirting the docklands, is not a popular destination. Tourists with only a few hours to spend will turn elsewhere. For Corvo, however, it had one abiding attraction:

> Today I have had adventures. This morning I bought a pair of boots and a kilogramme of tobacco. Lunched here, stewed celery, dry toast, water. Afterwards went to the Bonvecchiati, had a steak and a litre of red wine (the new vintage which is just in and very heady); and then, feeling up to any devilry, went smoking for a long walk through Cannareggio into the Ghetto to look for Jews. For mind you, a satisfactory Jew is worth a dozen Gentiles. They have more spunk about them somehow. I saw one whom I am going to watch as likely to be ready next spring. From here I got over to the station bridge and by a long round to the harbour end of the Zattere. A Sicilian ship was lying alongside the quay and armies of lusty youths

were dancing down long long planks with sacks on their shoulders which they delivered in a warehouse ashore. The air was filled with a cloud of fine white floury dust from the sacks which powdered the complexions of their carriers most deliciously and the fragrance of it was simply heavenly. As I stopped to look a minute one of the carriers attracted my notice. They were all half naked and sweating. I looked a second time as his face seemed familiar. He was running up a plank. And he also turned to look at me. Seeing my gaze he made me a sign for a cigarette. I grabbed at my pockets but hadn't got one; and shook my head. He ran on into the ship. I ran off to the nearest baccy shop and came back with a packet of cigs and a box of matches to wait at the foot of his plank. Presently he came down the plank dancing staggering under a sack. I watched him. Such a lovely figure, young, muscular, splendidly strong, big black eyes, rosy face, round black head, scented like an angel. As he came out again running (they are watched by guards all the time) I threw him my little offering. 'Who are you?' '*Amadeo Amadei*' (lovely mediaeval name). The next time, 'What are you carrying?' '*Lily-flowers for soap-making.*' The next time, 'Where have I seen you?' '*Assistant gondolier one day with Piero last year*' – then – '*Sir, Round Table* [a homosexual fraternity] –' My dear F. I'm going to that ship again to-morrow morning. I want to know more . . .[39]

PIAZZALE ROMA

From San Nicolò a short walk through the neglected western fringe of the city will bring us to the Piazzale Roma. It is perhaps not possible to step into the Piazzale itself without a lowering of the spirits – which is why it makes such a suitable point of departure from the city. With its waiting coaches, its smell of diesel, and the ugly mass of its prematurely dilapidated air terminal building, this dismal creation of the 1930s perfectly matches one's mood as one prepares to go back into the world.

Fortunately, our stay in Venice has only just begun. We have merely wandered out here to gloat, or perhaps returned from a brief excursion to what the seventeenth-century traveller James Howell refers to as 'the dainty Townes' of the plain. Standing at the edge of the Piazzale Roma, one has a sharper sense than anywhere else in Venice of all the disagreeable things that are left behind on stepping into the vaporetto or crossing the Rio Nuovo. To return by bus from a long day in Padua or Vicenza, to be dropped at this noisy terminus, and then simply to step away, leaving it behind, is a wonderful pleasure. A few seconds are all it takes to slip through one of the narrow openings that lead back into the city's fabulous cocoon.

Max Beerbohm catches exactly the sense of relief one feels on being returned to the embrace of Venice after contact with the harsher world outside. Having stayed in the city for some weeks, he begins to feel the edge of his appreciation dulled. It is time to leave, he thinks, before he runs the risk of surfeit.

One afternoon in Padua is enough to persuade him of his error. He wanders restlessly around the unfamiliar town: 'I turned down a side-street, under an arcade. All the side-streets seemed to be arcaded; and yes, they were picturesque; but how heavy, how coarse, in comparison with – no; it was not fair to make that comparison.' But the comparison keeps forcing itself upon him. He tries in vain to kill time. Finally, he seeks distraction at a theatre, and there his attention is caught by the struggles of a captive bird to escape the auditorium. It is a parable he takes to heart:

The manager of the hotel was very sorry I had to leave so soon; oh yes, there was a train for Venice: I should just have time to pack; he would have my bill made out at once.

It was a very slow train. My heart outran it a thousand times on the way. No lover was ever more impatient than I. No one had ever been more in love than I was. To think there were people who did not know Venice – people who had never yet lived! And those who did know her – did they know her as I did? No, she had told the secrets of her heart to me alone. She was waiting for me. I was on the way. . . .

I laughed aloud to myself, remembering my solemn academic theory about the dangers of sufficiency. I laughed to think that I had solemnly acted on this theory – prig and fool that I had been! Well, I had come to my senses. I could afford to laugh now. But why *wouldn't* the train go faster?

At last we were crossing the lagoon. And presently I was quit of the railway station, and out on the canal. There were scarves of cloud across the moon, and Venice looked more than ever visionary in that faint twilight. I felt not as though I had come to her in her sleep, but as though she, a vision, had come to me in mine; as though she, not I, were the 'revenant.' Was I truly awake? Yes, it was Venice that was sleeping. And '*Piano, gondoliere,*' I said. '*Lentamente . . . Piano . . .*'[40]

2

SAN POLO

SAN TOMÀ

'Sinking, Shadowed and Sad – The Last Glory of Europe' was
the title of a short newspaper piece on Venice which Evelyn
Waugh wrote in 1960. That the city was gradually and ineluct-
ably returning to the sea had by then become part of every
visitor's response to its melancholy beauty. Six years later the
November floods brought a devastating reality to this graceful
image.

Wherever one walks in Venice, wherever one lives, the
threat of encroaching water is never far away. There are days
in winter when the *diretto* which brushes past the stark façade
of San Pantalon on its way to the Grand Canal slops an angry
little wave across the paving-stones towards the church. And
on the other side of the Rio della Frescada, the Campo San
Tomà yields quickly to the rising waters at times of *acqua
alta*. When autumn winds bank up the waves beyond the
lagoon and the canals begin to swell, the local population has

learnt what to expect. Horatio Brown describes the familiar
sequence as he observed it at the end of the last century:

> Steadily the tide flows faster and faster under the bridge,
> and the market-men and gondoliers secure their boats to
> the posts. So it goes on for an hour or more, till the
> jade-coloured flood has nearly brimmed to the edge of the
> *fondamenta*, but not yet overflowed it. Then the water
> begins to appear in the calle; it comes welling up through
> every drain-hole and between the flags of the pavement,
> bubbling like a little geyser and making a low gurgling
> noise; for the sea begins to flood Venice under pavements,
> and not over the *fondamente*, which are usually higher than
> the streets. Presently the baker puts out a board to serve as
> a bridge for his customers; but soon the water from the
> canal has joined that in the calle; the bridge ceases to be of
> use, and floats idly away. . . . Then the first boat passes
> down the calle stopping at the shop doors to pick up fares,
> and bare-legged men offer their services as porters from
> the high bridge steps to the upper end of the street, which
> is still dry. Indeed, the flood is the excuse for the display of
> bare legs, and half the population of the quarter are tucked
> above the knee. All the windows are full of women and
> children, laughing at the traffic below. . . . Then sud-
> denly, without a moment's warning, there is a dazzling
> flash of lightning, a rattling peal; every face disappears
> from the windows, and all the green shutters go to with a
> bang.[1]

In a later age the disreputable artist who is the hero of one of
Malamud's stories makes a few lire by acting as a porter on
these occasions. It was perhaps here in the Campo San Tomà,
with its line of modest shops and its church full of relics, that
Fidelman took his stand, ferrying pedestrians piggy-back
across the underwater square:

> Fidelman waded in hip boots through high water glinting
> like shards of broken mirror in the freezing winter sun-
> light, and deposited his customers on dry ground whence
> they proceeded hurriedly along narrow streets and alleys.

Occasionally while transporting a female he gave her a modified feel along the leg, which roused no response through winter clothing; still it was good for the morale. One attractive, long-nosed, almost oriental-eyed young Venetian woman who mounted his back, began at once to giggle, and laughed, unable to control it, mirthfully as he slowly sloshed across the pond. She sat on Fidelman, enjoying the ride, her rump bumping his, cheek pressed to his frozen ear, hugging him casually, a pair of shapely black-stocking legs clasped in the crooks of his arms; and when he tenderly set her down, his penis erect, athrob, she kissed him affectionately and hastily went her way. As Fidelman watched she turned back, smiling sadly, as though they had once been lovers and the affair was ended. Then she waved goodbye and walked on. He wished she hadn't, for he was after a while in love with her.

When the water receded as the bora roared, drying the city, uncovering here and there a drowned cat, the winter light sprang up crystal clear as Fidelman, once more jobless, holding onto his hat – you can't chase them on the canals – sought his lady, to no avail. He searched from the Public Gardens to the Slaughter House and on both sides of the humpbacked Grand Canal. And he haunted the little square of blessed memory where he had once carried her across the wet water, chain smoking used butts from a pocketful in his overcoat as he watched a steam-breathed sweeper sweeping at the mud with a twig broom; but she never appeared.[2]

Fidelman does at length catch sight of his elusive passenger again, through a shop window in the Mercerie, but their subsequent affair, its course diverted by her husband, turns out to be less orthodox than he expects.

CASA GOLDONI

Beside the bridge which leads from the neighbouring Campiello San Tomà into the Calle dei Nomboli is a plaque indicating that this was the birthplace of the playwright Carlo Goldoni. 'I was born at Venice,' he writes in the opening sentence of his *Memoirs*, 'in the year 1707, in a large and beautiful house between the bridges of Nomboli and Donna Onestà, at the corner of the street Cà Centanni, in the parish of St Thomas.'[3]

Venice has attracted many writers from outside but produced few of its own. Even the Italians who are associated with it, like Aretino and d'Annunzio, tend to be settlers rather than natives. Goldoni is duly prized, and in a city that has never done much to honour its individual citizens his statue in the Campo San Bartolomeo is an unusual tribute. The Palazzo Centanni is in a picturesque area and is itself a handsome building. From a small courtyard with its own well-head an attractive stone staircase leads up to the first floor, where a room has been given over to the Goldoni Museum. Next to an entrance hall decorated with pictures of eighteenth-century Venice the main room houses a couple of costumes, some first editions, some commemorative medals, and a variety of engravings. As writers' museums go, the collection is unremarkable, but the fine setting and the scarcity of other visitors make it an agreeable spot to pass a few moments.

Santa Maria Gloriosa dei Frari

The advice handed down to generations of tourists has been to do the churches in the morning. You stand a chance of seeing what is inside them while the light is adequate and you sit down to lunch with a clear conscience. There is also the fact that certain churches close at midday and do not reopen. It may therefore seem perverse to recommend the winter evenings. But to walk through this part of Venice at about six o'clock, when the streets and campi are crowded with evening shoppers wrapped against the cold, can be a pleasure as keen as any that Venice offers. Dark alleys open into brightly lit squares, narrow canals catch patches of light from windows in the flaking walls, simple shops acquire a seductive glow that transforms their daytime ordinariness.

It is not just the bridges and canals and the dream-like architecture that create this atmosphere. The shops themselves belong in part to an earlier age. Many of them have no names or only the discreetest lettering above the door. Their windows are recessed, sometimes under eaves, often set in thick walls. It is the sort of display that in England can only be found on a tiny scale in villages bypassed by the march of neon.

This time of evening lends a curious thrill to what might otherwise be the routine business of visiting another church. The smoking candles and the softness of the light on the other side of the church-door offer the giddy experience of slipping from one world to another.

This is especially true of the Frari. Those who find it hard to love the church by day should try it now. There are disadvantages, of course. Here, as elsewhere, the statuary recedes, its outlines muffled in shade; details of art and architecture become harder to distinguish. But such drawbacks are partial. Against them it might be urged that much ecclesiastical sculpture can only benefit from a little kindly shade. Canova's tomb in the north aisle is a case in point – at least according to Ruskin: 'The tomb of Canova, *by* Canova, cannot be missed; consummate in science, intolerable in affectation, ridiculous in conception, null and void to the uttermost in invention and feeling.'[4] After which, the wretched sculptor might well wish it in perpetual shade.

Directly to the right of the main door is the attractive sixteenth-century monument to Pietro Bernardo, an otherwise undistinguished scion of the patrician family which gave its name to a number of the city's streets. Rising in stately marble tiers, it looks to most visitors a fairly handsome memorial, but Pietro himself, who died in 1538, would hardly have been satisfied. The terms of his will, drawn up well in advance on 30 October 1515, make it quite clear what he had in mind:

> His instructions were that as soon as he was dead his body should be washed in the finest vinegar and then anointed with musk to the value of 40 ducats by three of the most renowned doctors, each of whom would receive in

payment 3 fine, newly minted *zecchini*; that he should then be laid with aloes and other spices in a coffin of lead which had room enough for his body to lie at ease. This should then be enclosed in another, extremely large coffin of cypress wood, so well sealed and fastened that it could not be opened without being broken into. This to be then placed in a marble tomb to the value of 600 ducats, on the front of which should be carved 8 verses rehearsing his deeds in capital letters large enough to be read at a distance of 25 feet, the poet to be paid a zecchino for every two verses. Above the tomb should be carved the Eternal Father and a likeness of Pietro Bernardo himself kneeling, the image to be large enough for him to appear, at a distance of 25 feet, a man of tall stature. Finally, it was prescribed that the glories of his family should be celebrated in a book of 800 verses. In addition, seven psalms should be composed in imitation of the Psalms of David, together with other prayers, these to be sung by twenty friars on the first Sunday of every month, at day-break, in front of his sepulchre.[5]

Before moving on to San Rocco, note the monastery buildings beside the main door of the Frari. In over three hundred rooms they house the voluminous archives of State. It was here that Rawdon Brown spent the last twenty years of his life, examining, it is said, some twelve million packets of documents in order to calendar the state papers that related to British history.

SCUOLA GRANDE DI SAN ROCCO

The attractions of the Scuola di San Rocco, a few yards from the Frari, were bluntly summed up by Gilbert Burnet at the end of the seventeenth century: 'The School of Sant. Roch, and the Chappel, and Hall are full of great pieces of Tintorets.' On the young John Ruskin their effect was more dramatic. 'I have been quite overwhelmed today,' he wrote to his father on 23 September 1845, 'by a man whom I never dreamed of –

Tintoret.' Next day he went back to study the paintings in
more detail:

> I have had a draught of pictures today enough to drown
> me. I never was so utterly crushed to the earth before any
> human intellect as I was today, before Tintoret. Just be so
> good as to take my list of painters, & put him in the school
> of Art at the top, top, top of everything, with a great big
> black line underneath him to stop him off from every-
> body – and put him in the school of Intellect, next after
> Michael Angelo. He took it so entirely out of me today
> that I could do nothing at last but lie on a bench &
> laugh. . . . Tintoret don't seem to be able to stretch
> himself till you give him a canvas forty feet square – &
> then, he lashes out like a leviathan, and heaven and earth
> come together. M Angelo himself cannot hurl figures
> into space as he does, nor did M Angelo ever paint space
> itself which would not look like a nutshell beside
> Tintoret's. Just imagine the audacity of the fellow – in his
> massacre of the innocents one of the mothers has hurled
> herself off a terrace to avoid the executioner & is falling
> headforemost & backwards, holding up the child still.
> And such a resurrection as there is – the rocks of the
> sepulchre crashed all to pieces & roaring down upon you,
> while the Christ soars forth into a torrent of angels,
> whirled up into heaven till you are lost ten times over.
> And then to see his touch of quiet thought in his awful
> crucifixion – there is an *ass* in the distance, feeding on the
> remains of strewed palm leaves. If that isn't a master's
> stroke, I don't know what is.[6]

That tourists now stream through San Rocco on their round
of the city's sights is partly due to these two days in September
1845. For the modern visitor the paintings are reasonably lit,
but the experience is perhaps a little comfortless. Less than one
might wish remains of the atmosphere described by Henry
James in 1882:

> The interest, the impressiveness, of that whole corner of
> Venice, however melancholy the effect of its gorgeous

and ill-lighted chambers, gives a strange importance to a visit to the Scuola. Nothing that all travellers go to see appears to suffer less from the incursions of travellers. It is one of the loneliest booths of the bazaar, and the author of these lines has always had the good fortune, which he wishes to every other traveller, of having it to himself. I think most visitors find the place rather alarming and wicked-looking. They walk about a while among the fitful figures that gleam here and there out of the great tapestry (as it were) with which the painter has hung all the walls, and then, depressed and bewildered by the portentous solemnity of these objects, by strange glimpses of unnatural scenes, by the echo of their lonely footsteps on the vast stone floors, they take a hasty departure, finding themselves again, with a sense of release from danger, a sense that the *genius loci* was a sort of mad white-washer who worked with a bad mixture, in the bright light of the *campo*, among the beggars, the orange-vendors and the passing gondolas. Solemn indeed is the place, solemn and strangely suggestive, for the simple reason that we shall scarcely find four walls elsewhere that inclose within a like area an equal quantity of genius. The air is thick with it and dense and difficult to breathe; for it was genius that was not happy, inasmuch as it lacked the art to fix itself for ever. It is not immortality that we breathe at the Scuola di San Rocco, but conscious, reluctant mortality.[7]

St Roch himself, a Frenchman who devoted the last part of his life to nursing victims of the Black Death, had originally been venerated in Montpellier, until one of the Republic's pious thefts brought him to Venice. His sarcophagus now rests in the church.

PONTE DELLA LATE

From San Rocco it is worth a short detour via the Calle Dietro l'Archivio and the Corte Vitalba to the enticing Scuola di San Giovanni Evangelista. 'Beautiful it is, even in its squalid misery,' writes Ruskin. 'As long as it is let alone, in its shafts and capitals you will see on the whole the most characteristic example in Venice of the architecture that Carpaccio, Cima, and John Bellini loved.'[8]

Since we are now heading for San Agostin, it is no more than a whim that makes us turn left up the Calle dell'Olio to the Ponte della Late. This is not a celebrated bridge, and there is no reason why it should be. It is merely the site of one of those bizarre incidents with which Venetian history is crammed – the sort of thing that in most places is forgotten but that in Venice is preserved in the literary byways of its diarists and antiquarians. While Carpaccio's languid courtiers strolled at large through the city, Marin Sanudo, a learned patrician salaried by the Council of Ten, was compiling an extraordinary survey of the world that passed before their eyes. In the fifty-eight volumes of his diary he recorded the minutiae of Venetian life, both public and private, with a sharp eye for the dramatic, the scabrous, and the grotesque. On 31 August 1505 he notes:

> Today the execution took place of the Albanian who treacherously murdered Zuan Marco. First, his hand was cut off at the Ponte della Late. And mark that this gave rise to a curious incident; to wit, while his wife was taking leave of him, he made as if he wanted to kiss her and bit her nose off. It is said that she was responsible for bringing his crime to light.[9]

THE ALDINE PRESS

Opposite the gateway of the Scuola, the Calle Zane, entered through a narrow archway, leads us towards the slightly battered, quiet little square of San Agostin. This was once the site of the palace of Baiamonte Tiepolo. In 1310 Baiamonte had been at the head of an uprising to depose the Doge. When it failed, his palace was destroyed and replaced by a *colonna d'infamia*, which was later removed to the Correr Museum. Beside the clothes shop on the corner of the Calle della Chiesa, you will see in the place where the column once stood a cracked paving-stone bearing the inscription *Loc. Col. Bai. The. MCCCX.*

We can leave the square by the Rio Terrà Seconda. At no. 2311, a few yards along on the right-hand side, stands a small Gothic palace with a pleasant balcony round the three central windows on the second floor. This was the home of one of the great printing presses of the Renaissance.

By the end of the fifteenth century, Venice's two hundred printers had issued more works than Rome, Florence, and Milan put together. Although the press here was not entirely free, it was at least protected from the worst of the Church's meddling. Most famous of the Venetian presses was that of Aldus Manutius. Under the imprint of the dolphin and anchor, it quickly became known for its fine editions of the classics, and when Erasmus wanted a publisher for his enlarged edition of the *Adagia*, it was to Aldus that he turned.

Having reached Venice in the spring of 1508, Erasmus spent the rest of the year in the home of Aldus's father-in-law, Andrea Torresani. The resulting collaboration was successful enough from a literary point of view, but in other respects Erasmus found life in the Torresani household something of an ordeal. Twenty years later, in 'Opulentia Sordida', he produced a rancorous satire on the family's domestic arrangements. What dismayed him most, apart from the bugs and fleas, was the miserly provision of food: watered wine, mouldy bread, small leaves of lettuce swimming in vinegar, cheese as hard as stone, soup fit for sows. In the end, Erasmus claims, he was forced to fend for himself:

> I employ'd a certain Friend to buy me every Day three Eggs with my own Money, two for my Dinner, and one for my Supper: But here also the Women put their Tricks upon me; for instead of my new-laid Eggs that I paid a good Price for, they would give me rotten ones, that I thought I came well off, if one of my three Eggs prov'd eatable. I also at last got a small Cask of good Wine bought for my own drinking, but the Women broke open my Cellar-Door, and in a few Days drank it all up,

and my Landlord *Antronius* did not seem to be much displeas'd at the Matter.[10]

Fortunately, perhaps, by the time this sketch of Venetian hospitality appeared in print, Aldus himself was long dead.

Campo San Polo

Just beyond the Aldine Press, the Calle del Scaleter leads down towards the vast Campo San Polo, the biggest square in Venice after St Mark's. Its size has made it a natural site for festivities, from bull-fights in the seventeenth century to open-air discothèques in the modern carnival. In earlier times one of the more notable episodes was the great bonfire of vanities held here on 26 July 1450 at the urging of a Franciscan friar who was a follower of Bernardine of Siena. Fripperies, fine clothes, and false coils of hair all went up in flames at a jamboree that anticipated the efforts of Savonarola in Florence forty years later. But these displays of religious enthusiasm were not really to the Venetians' taste, and they soon returned to a preference for more secular entertainments of the sort described by John Evelyn in 1646. Deep snow had kept him in Padua through January, but he managed to leave in time for Shrove Tuesday, 'when all the world repaire to *Venice* to see the folly & madnesse of the *Carnevall*':

> The Women, Men & persons of all Conditions disguising themselves in antique dresses, & extravagant Musique & a thousand gambols, & traversing the streetes from house to house, all places being then accessible, & free to enter: There is abroad nothing but flinging of Eggs fill'd with sweete Waters, & sometimes not over sweete; they also have a barbarous costome of hunting bulls about the Streetes & Piazzas, which is very dangerous, the passages being generally so narrow in that Citty: Likewise do the youth of the severall Wards & parrishes contend in other Masteries or pastimes, so as tis altogether impossible to recount the universal madnesse of this place during this time of licence: Now are the greate banks set up for those

who will play at Basset, the Comedians have also liberty
& the *Operas* to exercise: Witty pasquils are likewise
thrown about, & the Mountebanks have their stages in
every Corner.[11]

The festive traditions of the Campo San Polo have not been
without problems for the church at the south-west corner. If
you walk round to the wall of the apse, you will see an early
bas-relief of the Madonna with saints and angels. Under it is a
square stone plaque set there in 1611, of which Captain
Douglas offers a rough translation:

> MDCXI. 10th August. All games whatsoever are pro-
> hibited: as also the sales of goods, or the erection of shops,
> round this church, by order of the most excellent
> 'esecutori contra la biastema' [magistrates appointed for
> the suppression of blasphemy, swearing and kindred
> offences]: with the penalty of prison, the galleys, exile,
> and also 300 lire de' piccoli, to be divided between the
> accuser and captors.[12]

Noble festivities were perhaps viewed with a different eye.
It was a private celebration in the Palazzo Soranzo, at the east
end of the square, that marked a turning point in the career of
Giacomo Casanova. Educated to a profession in the church, he
had slipped into a life of hectic dissipation, making what
money he could as a hired musician and living by night in wild
and vicious company. It was at this point, around the time of
his twenty-first birthday, that he met the man who was to
become his principal friend and protector in Venice. Senator
Matteo Giovanni Bragadin was a decent, rather gullible patrician whose name would have been long forgotten if a brush
with death had not brought him into contact with Casanova.
In the spring of 1746 Casanova was one of the musicians
playing at the celebrations for the marriage of Girolamo
Cornaro with a daughter of the Soranzo family:

> On the third day, when the festivities were nearly over, I
> leave the orchestra an hour before dawn to go home, and
> as I go downstairs I notice a senator in his red robe about
> to get into his gondola. I see a letter drop to the ground

beside him as he is drawing his handkerchief from his pocket. I advance and pick up the letter and, catching up with the imposing Signore just as he is going down the steps, I hand it to him. He thanks me, he asks me where I live, I tell him, he insists upon taking me home, I accept the courtesy he was kind enough to offer me, and take a place on the bench beside him. Three minutes later he asks me to shake his left arm: 'I feel,' he said, 'such a numbness that I seem not to have this arm at all.' I shake it with all my might, and I hear him tell me, in ill-articulated words, that he felt as if he were losing his whole leg too and that he thought he was dying.

Greatly alarmed, I open the curtain, take the lantern, look at his face, and am terrified to see that his mouth was drawn up towards his left ear and his eyes were losing their lustre.

I call to the gondoliers to stop and let me get out to find a surgeon who will come at once and bleed His Excellency, who had certainly been struck by apoplexy.

I disembark. It was at the bridge by the Calle Bernardo, where three years earlier I had given Razzetta a cudgeling. I run to the coffeehouse, someone shows me where a surgeon lives. I knock loudly, I shout, the door opens, the man is wakened, I urge him to hurry, I will not let him dress, he takes his case and comes with me to the gondola, where he bleeds the dying man, and I tear up my shirt to make him a bandage.

We quickly reach his palace in Santa Marina; the servants are awakened, he is removed from his gondola, carried to his apartment on the second floor, undressed, and put to bed almost dead. I tell a servant to run for a physician, he goes, the physician arrives and bleeds him again. I station myself beside the bed, considering it my duty not to leave.[13]

Bragadin survived to be grateful. It was for Casanova the start of a valuable friendship.

MURDER OF LORENZINO

Almost exactly two hundred years earlier the square had witnessed a murder which was both elaborately planned and extravagantly rewarded. At the far end of the campo, just between the campanile and the southern doorway of the church, is the spot where Lorenzino de' Medici was assassinated in 1546. It is an intriguing episode that gives a sharp edge of reality to some of the traditional clichés about life in Renaissance Italy.

The story is graphically told by J. A. Symonds from the record left by one of the murderers. Nine years earlier Lorenzino had himself been responsible for the murder of his cousin Alessandro, who was then Duke of Florence. As the next Duke of Florence, Cosimo de' Medici was concerned that this should not become a precedent. He was a serious man, and the price he put on Lorenzino's head was vast.[14] Before long two soldiers of fortune called Bebo and Bibboni had managed to track Lorenzino to Venice. Symonds takes up the narrative, using Bibboni's own account:

> In the carnival of 1546 Lorenzo meant to go masked in the habit of a gypsy woman to the square of San Spirito, where there was to be a joust. Great crowds of people would assemble, and Bibboni hoped to do his business there. The assassination, however, failed on this occasion, and Lorenzo took up his abode in the palace he had hired upon the Campo di San Polo. This Campo is one of the largest open places in Venice, shaped irregularly, with a finely curving line upon the western side, where two of the noblest private houses in the city are still standing. Nearly opposite these, in the south-western angle, stands detached, the little old church of San Polo. One of its side-entrances opens upon the square; the other on a lane which leads eventually to the Frari. There is nothing in Bibboni's narrative to make it clear where Lorenzo hired his dwelling. But it would seem from certain things which he says later on, that in order to enter the church his victim had to cross the square. Meanwhile Bibboni took the precaution of making friends with a shoe maker,

whose shop commanded the whole Campo, including Lorenzo's palace. In this shop he began to spend much of his time; 'and oftentimes I feigned to be asleep; but God knows whether I was sleeping, for my mind, at any rate, was wide-awake.'[15]

After weeks of observation the assassins finally get their chance. On 28 February 1546 Lorenzo and his bodyguard cross the square in company with a third man, Alessandro Soderini, and enter the church. Bebo, on watch at the southern door, opposite the campanile, sees them push aside the thick leather curtain and signals to Bibboni. When Lorenzo emerges from the southern door, Bibboni is waiting:

I saw him issue from the church and take the main street; then came Alessandro Soderini, and I walked last of all; and when we reached the point we had determined on, I jumped in front of Alessandro with the poignard in my hand, crying, 'Hold hard, Alessandro, and get along with you, in God's name, for we are not here for you!' He then threw himself around my waist, and grasped my arms, and kept on calling out. Seeing how wrong I had been to try to spare his life, I wrenched myself as well as I could from his grip, and with my lifted poignard struck him, as God willed, above the eyebrow, and a little blood trickled from the wound. He, in high fury, gave me such a thrust that I fell backward, and the ground beside was slippery from having rained a little. Then Alessandro drew his sword, which he carried in its scabbard, and thrust at me in front, and struck me on the corslet, which for my good fortune was of double mail. Before I could get ready I received three passes, which, had I worn a doublet instead of that mailed corslet, would certainly have run me through. At the fourth pass I had regained my strength and spirit, and closed with him, and stabbed him four times in the head, and being so close he could not use his sword, but tried to parry with his hand and hilt, and I, as God willed, struck him at the wrist below the sleeve of mail, and cut his hand off clean, and gave him then one last stroke on his head. Thereupon he begged for God's sake spare his life, and I, in trouble about Bebo, left him in the arms of a Venetian nobleman, who held him back from jumping in the canal. . . .

When I turned, I found Lorenzo on his knees. He raised himself, and I, in anger, gave him a great cut across the head, which split it in two pieces, and laid him at my feet, and he never rose again.[16]

There follows a breathless chase across Venice until the two assassins finally take refuge in the Spanish embassy, from which some days later they are smuggled out to the mainland via the Cannaregio canal. Once at Pisa they are safe. As Bibboni smugly remarks, 'We were now able for the whole time of life left us to live splendidly, without a thought or care.' Renaissance Italy knew little of the code by which evil fails to prosper. Bibboni concludes his narrative with the words: 'Bebo from Pisa, at what date I know not, went home to Volterra, his native town, and there finished his days; while I abode in Florence, where I have had no further wish to hear of wars, but to live my life in holy peace.'

Palazzo Corner Mocenigo

At the far end of the square from the church, at nos 2128 and 2128a, stands the massive Palazzo Corner Mocenigo. Since the eighteenth century two doors from it have opened on to the Campo San Polo, an arrangement ordered by Giovanni Cornaro so that the dead and the living might never pass through the same doorway. Corvo stayed here from the summer of 1909 to the spring of the following year as a guest of the Van Someren family, and it was from here that he wrote most of the notorious Venice letters, detailing his exploits, real or imagined, with the lithe gondoliers for whom he pined. His memories of the palace were not happy. Looking at the rather bleak face of the Campo San Polo on a December afternoon, one can imagine something of the rigours of a bad winter:

The fact is this last fortnight has been absolutely Devilish. No tobacco, Alps covered with snow, *bora* blowing up Adriatic one day and wind from Alps bringing simply perishing cold. And here I live and work and sleep on an *open landing* of this palace on the side which never sees the sun with *stone* floor, walls, ceiling and stairs, no privacy (it's the servants' stair) and *no heating arrangements whatever*. My dear, *I'm simply dying of cold and hunger*. The doctor is a dear. If he didn't give me this hospitality I should be on the streets and that would be the end of all my hopes.[17]

This charitable view of Dr Van Someren did not last. On 28 December Corvo writes:

As for me, things have gone from bad to worse. I have never had such an unchristian Christmas in my life. Never! Neither beef nor turkey nor plum-pudding nor mince-pie have passed my lips, and I ADORE them all. Not a single soul said or sent a single Christmas word to me excepting the servants here and the boys. No, not one. . . . Our dear pious Plymouth Brother of a doctor dismissed three of his six servants when I last wrote to you, the man and two maids: and shunted on to me their work which I have been doing ever since. This gets me up at 5.30 to light fires, fill cisterns, work the cream-making machine, and get up wood for the stoves. It's devilish hard work. . . . Of course my book is at a standstill. How can I possibly write when I'm toiling upstairs bent double with a load of wood, much less think out what I'm going to write with my mind raging in agony and disappointment?[18]

Hospitality to Rolfe was always likely to earn mixed rewards. The book in question was *The Desire and Pursuit of the Whole*. When the Van Somerens discovered it to be a scarcely veiled attack on their friends in the English colony, the troublesome author was asked to leave.

RIO DI SAN APONAL

To get from the Campo San Polo to the Campiello Albrizzi takes only a couple of minutes, but it is one of the most fascinating walks in the city. The succession of twisting alleys, empty canals, dark corners, and crumbling arcades offers one in the space of a few yards a stretch of quintessential Venice. Late in the afternoon, beside the lonely Rio di San Aponal, the air seems haunted – perhaps by the romantic couple who pass this way in Carlo Gozzi's autobiography.

Gozzi himself, the only serious rival of Goldoni on the eighteenth-century stage, was if anything a somewhat moralistic figure, different from Casanova in almost every way; and yet the Venice that emerges from their memoirs is in some respects uncannily similar. As a young man Gozzi had become acquainted with the attractive girl who lived opposite him in the Calle della Regina (see p. 59). From time to time her melancholy songs had drifted through his study window and the two had moved from exchanging bows to exchanging words – no further. But she was the young wife of an impotent old aristocrat and this acquaintance with Gozzi was seized on by her husband's unscrupulous lodgers as a means of extorting money from her. In desperation she turned to Gozzi for help:

She had obtained her husband's permission to go that day after dinner to visit an aunt of hers, a nun, on the Giudecca. Therefore she begged me to repair at twenty-one o'clock to the *sotto portico* by the *ponte storto* at S. Aponal. There I should see, waiting or arriving, a gondola with a white handkerchief hung out of one of its windows. I was to get boldly into this gondola, and I should find her inside. 'Then you will hear all about the circumstances in which my want of caution has involved me.' . . .

I took my dinner in haste, nearly choked myself, and alleging business of the last importance, flew off to the *ponte storto*. The gondola was in position at a *riva*, with the flag of the white handkerchief hung out. I entered it in haste, impelled perhaps by the desire to join the lovely woman, perhaps by curiosity to hear her explanation. When I entered, there she was, resplendent with gems of price at her ears, her throat, her fingers, underneath the *zendado*. She made room for me beside her, and gave orders to the gondolier that he should draw the curtain, and row toward the Giudecca to a monastery which she named.[19]

Gozzi manages to extricate her from the blackmailers but in the process becomes himself entangled with her. Their affair ends unhappily, though not the rest of the girl's story. In time her ailing husband dies and she can marry a respectable merchant, making thereafter, Gozzi informs us, a model wife.

A short way along the arcaded fondamenta beside the Rio di San Aponal we can turn left down the narrowest street of all, the Calle Stretta, into the Campiello Albrizzi. Just opposite the calle, between the ground floor windows of no. 1491, is a fragment of Austrian shell with beside it d'Annunzio's ringing declaration, one of his many:

> This fragment of barbarism is lodged in the noble stone as testimony of the perpetual enmity which adds shame to their shame, glory to our glory. 10 August 1916.

Ponte Storto

At the far end of the campiello the Calle Albrizzi leads back to the lovely Ponte Storto. On the left, facing the canal, is the splendidly dilapidated old house which was the home of Bianca Cappello. It was from one of these balconies that in 1563 she made the acquaintance of a Florentine bank-clerk who was living in a nearby house. She was only fifteen at the time and the youth was well below her in rank. Their subsequent elopement caused her father enough dismay for him to have them both declared outlaws.

Life in Florence with the clerk and his family quickly proved tiresome, but Bianca had the good fortune to come to the notice of Francesco de' Medici, son of the Grand Duke of Tuscany. Over the next few years the deaths of Bianca's husband, Francesco's father, and finally, in 1578, Francesco's wife left the outlaw from Venice in the position of Grand Duchess of Tuscany. Pragmatic as ever, the Venetians pronounced her a 'true and particular Daughter of the Republic', and for the next eight years she repaid the courtesy by doing all she could to forward Venetian interests. Sadly, when she and Francesco died within a couple of days of each other, either from poison or disease, Venice left her unmourned and made no attempt to recover the body which the hatred of Francesco's brother had consigned to a common grave. Popular legend has been kinder, and today her house is marked by a plaque.

The place is a match for its romantic history. With crumbling stonework eaten away around the windows and a few simple plants overhanging the balcony, it looks altogether in keeping with its past. The atmosphere of this charmed region of the city is caught by George Sand in the second of her *Lettres d'un voyageur*:

> Do you remember the little light that glimmers at the far end of the canal and is reflected and multiplied in the shining weather-worn marble of Bianca Cappello's house? There is not a more mysterious and melancholy little canal in all of Venice. That single light shining on all things and lighting none, dancing on the water and seeming to play in the wake of a passing boat like a will-o'-the-wisp bent on pursuing it, reminded me of that long row of street-lamps quivering in the Seine and tracing fiery zigzags upon its waters.[20]

CALLE DEL STURION

From the Ponte Storto we can carry straight on to the church of Sant'Aponal and then turn left along the Ruga Vecchia San Giovanni in the direction of the Rialto. About a hundred yards before the bridge, an opening on the right leads into the Calle del Sturion. The street takes its name from a celebrated inn, the Sturgeon, which for many years stood here on the corner of the Fondamenta del Vin. By 1398 it is already mentioned in the city records for watering its wine.

The commercial importance of the Rialto made it a prime site for inns. Through the fourteenth and fifteenth centuries a stream of pilgrims stayed in this district on their way to the

Holy Land (see p. 183). In 1436 the Spanish traveller Pero Tafur notes arriving in Venice and going straight to worship in St Mark's, 'after which we went to an inn called the *Sturgeon*, a very notable hostelry, where we lodged the day and night following'.[21] By chance this is the same inn which found its way into Carpaccio's painting of the *Miracle of the Holy Cross* about sixty-five years later. If you look closely at the left-hand side of the picture, you can see its sign, with a silver fish on a red background, just above the projecting porch in front of the old Rialto bridge.

The annual rent paid by a landlord in this favoured area could be as much as 800 ducats, 250 more than for some of the best palaces in the city. The inn had to make a corresponding profit, and landlords were not always scrupulous about how this was achieved. As long as the State was overseeing the pilgrim trade, foreigners could expect to be reasonably well treated, but later visitors had harsh things to say of the standards of Italian inns, and Venice was not excepted. Samuel Sharp, a surgeon from Guy's Hospital, delivered what had become by the middle of the eighteenth century a familiar broadside:

There are, by the bye, no such things as curtains, and hardly, from *Venice* to *Rome*, that cleanly and most useful invention, a privy; so that what should be collected and buried in oblivion, is for ever under your nose and eyes. Take along with you, that in all these inns the walls are bare, and the floor has never once been washed since it was first laid. One of the most indelicate customs here, is, that men, and not women, make the Ladies beds, and would do every office of a maid servant, if suffered. To sum up, in a word, the total of *Italian* nastiness, your chamber, which you would wish to be the sweetest, is by far the most offensive room in the house, for reasons I shall not explain. I must tell you, that except in two or three places, they never scour their pewter, and unless you were to see it, you will not conceive how dirty and nauseous it grows in thirty or forty years. Their knives are of the same colour as their pewter, and their table-

cloths and napkins such as you see on joint-stools, in
Bartholomew-Fair, where the mob eat their sausages. In
these inns they make you pay largely, so much a head, and
send up ten times as much as you can eat. For example,
this is almost constantly the fare. – A soop like wash, with
pieces of liver swimming in it; a plate full of brains, fried
in the shape of fritters; a dish of livers and gizzards; a
couple of fowls (always killed after your arrival) boiled to
rags, without any the least kind of sauce, or herbage;
another fowl, just killed, stewed as they call it; then two
more fowl, or a turkey roasted to rags. . . . The bread all
the way is exceedingly bad, and the butter so rancid, it
cannot be touched, or even borne within the reach of our
smell.[22]

Venice is still not a wonderful place for food, but things
have improved.

RIALTO

From whatever direction one approaches the Rialto, the press
of people on the streets increases. Four centuries before
Shylock it was already the commercial heart of the city, and
four centuries later it is still the most crowded place in Venice.
The Ruga degli Orefici, at the centre of this district, is the old
street of goldsmiths, whose business was confined to the
Rialto by a law of the fourteenth century. In 1594, at about the
time Shakespeare's thoughts were turning to Venice, Fynes
Moryson was making his way through Italy on the last leg of
his long European journey. A surprising amount of what he
observed around the Rialto will be familiar to the modern
visitor:

The foure square market place of Rialto, is compassed
with publike houses, under the arches whereof, and in the
middle part lying open, the Merchants meet. And there is
also a peculiar place where the Gentlemen meet before
noone, as they meet in the place of Saint Marke towards
evening. . . . The Gold-smiths shoppes lie thereby, and
over against them the shoppes of Jewellers, in which Art

the Venetians are excellent. There is the Pallace of a Gentleman, who proving a Traytor, the State (for his reproch) turned the same into a shambles, and some upper chambers to places of judgement. The fish market lies by this shambles, a great length along the banke of the great channell, and in the same shambles and fish market, as also in the like of Saint Marke, great plenty of victuals, especially of fish, is daily to be sold.[23]

It was here, amid a scene which impressed itself on generations of English writers, that Antonio walked in *The Merchant of Venice* and Otway's conspirators plotted revolution in *Venice Preserved*.

The bridge of the Rialto has had a mixed press. In the judgement of the Venetians, says Moryson, it 'deserves to be reputed the eighth miracle of the world'. Coryate, while deploring 'the vicious and licentious varlets' who worked the traghetto underneath it, was in agreement – 'the fairest bridge by many degrees for one arch that ever I saw, read, or heard of.' But then both Moryson and Coryate were there within a few years of the bridge's completion. Others have since been less charitable, condemning it as top-heavy and ungraceful. The dispute is academic. Like the Eiffel Tower, the Rialto has acquired a symbolic status that puts it well beyond the reach of aesthetic judgements.

Walking back from the bridge, we pass Venice's oldest church, San Giacomo di Rialto, now almost entirely obscured by sellers of trinkets, vegetables, and the inevitable Murano glass. Some way further on, the Ruga degli Speziali runs into the little Campo delle Beccarie. The Beccarie are the shambles referred to by Moryson, created in the early fourteenth century as a reprisal against the Quirini family for their part in the revolt of Baiamonte Tiepolo. The vengeance of the Republic has been long-lasting: today the lively square is still pervaded winter and summer by the smell of fish. For the enthusiast, of course, the proximity of the market is not necessarily a penance. The light of a Venetian dawn, writes Elizabeth David, 'is so limpid and so still that it makes every separate vegetable and fruit and fish luminous with a life of its own, with unnaturally heightened colours and clear stencilled outlines':

> In other markets, on other shores, the unfamiliar fishes may be vivid, mysterious, repellent, fascinating, and bright with splendid colour; only in Venice do they look good enough to eat. In Venice even ordinary sole and ugly great skate are striped with delicate lilac lights, the sardines shine like newly-minted silver coins, pink Venetian *scampi* are fat and fresh, infinitely enticing in the early dawn.[24]

SAN CASSIANO

A couple of minutes from the Campo delle Beccarie, on the far side of the adjacent canal, is the Campo San Cassiano. We are now in the midst of what was for long the most notorious area of the city. From the fifteenth century onwards it was a rare traveller who could return without commenting on the number and beauty of the Venetian courtesans. 'The best flesh-shambles in Italy', Venice was called in John Day's *Humour out of Breath*, and the city's name, with its mingled suggestions of the exotic and the erotic, has graced brothels across the world from sixteenth-century Whitefriars to twentieth-century Bangkok.

Tradition has long outlived reality; if people wish to sin in Venice today, they take their own company. By contrast, provision for earlier travellers was often felt by the authorities to be excessive. In 1439 an attempt had been made to confine women of the town to the area called Castelletto, allowing them by day to ply their trade around the streets and inns towards the Rialto; but gradually they began to colonize the district of San Cassiano, and it is with this part of the city, known at the time as Carampane, that they came to be associated.

The reputation of the area can be judged by the dispassionate details of the State archives on prostitution. It matters little which page one opens: 'Elena, Courtesan, lives in San Cassiano in the Corte della Ruosa, fined 30 ducats, 5 May

1581.' The entry is typical. Today the square itself is in every way a modest enough spot, though if you glance down the Calle dei Morti or pause before the somewhat dissolute buildings which front the canal on the far side of the campo, it is not difficult to imagine the world that Thomas Coryate stepped into in 1608.

Stepped is the appropriate word. An eccentric Englishman from Odcombe in Somerset, Coryate had made a good part of the journey to Venice on foot. He paid his respects to the British ambassador, Sir Henry Wotton, and also, at some length, to the courtesans:

> As for the number of these Venetian Cortezans it is very great. For it is thought there are of them in the whole City and other adjacent places, as Murano, Malamocco, & c. at the least twenty thousand, whereof many are esteemed so loose, that they are said to open their quivers to every arrow. A most ungodly thing without doubt that there should be a tolleration of such licentious wantons in so glorious, so potent, so renowned a city. For me thinks that the Venetians should be dailie affraid least their winking at such uncleannesse should be an occasion to draw down upon them Gods curse and vengeance from heaven, and to consume their city with fire and brimstone, as in times past he did Sodome and Gomorrha.[25]

But the Venetians were a practical lot, and the fear of divine retribution was held at bay by more pressing concerns. The number and variety of prostitutes made Venetian husbands feel more secure against the danger of being, in Coryate's phrase, 'capricornified' and also supplied the State with enough tax revenue to maintain a dozen galleys.

In spite of a succession of sumptuary laws, the luxury with which the more successful Italian courtesans surrounded themselves was a subject of frequent comment by contemporary travellers. So overwhelmed was a Spanish ambassador in the sixteenth century that rather than soil the rugs and hangings around him, he chose, with a delicacy that did him credit, to spit on to the face of one of his valets.[26]

Coryate was plainly entranced:

For so infinite are the allurements of these amorous
Calypsoes, that the fame of them hath drawn many to
Venice from some of the remotest parts of Christendome,
to contemplate their beauties, and enjoy their pleasing
dalliances. And indeede such is the variety of the delicious
objects they minister to their lovers, that they want
nothing tending to delight. For when you come into one
of their Palaces . . . you seem to enter into the Paradise of
Venus. For their fairest roomes are most glorious and
glittering to behold. The walles round about being
adorned with most sumptuous tapistry and gilt
leather . . .[27]

But pleasure must be paid, and the Venetian courtesan had a
sharp way with defaulters:

Moreover I will tell thee this newes which is most true,
that if thou shouldest wantonly converse with her, and
not give her that salarium iniquitatis, which thou hast
promised her, but perhaps cunningly escape from her
company, shee will either cause thy throate to be cut by
her Ruffiano, if he can after catch thee in the City, or
procure thee to be arrested (if thou art to be found) and
clapped up in the prison, where thou shalt remaine till
thou hast paid her all thou didst promise her.[28]

The pragmatic attitude of the Venetian State towards its
prostitutes is nicely illustrated by one of the more bizarre
edicts of the fifteenth century, reported by Gallicciolli. In an
effort to wean the youth of Venice from sodomy, it was
decreed that the city's courtesans, when sitting at the window
to attract clients, should leave their breasts uncovered. (Hence
the name of the nearby Ponte delle Tette.) How much success
the measure enjoyed is doubtful; the logic of the situation
might suggest that it would have been better to keep everything covered for as long as possible. Indeed, some of the more
enterprising courtesans had the wit to improve their chances
by dressing as young men.

At all events, the problem was one which continued to
exercise the Senate, as a series of other edicts in the fifteenth

and sixteenth centuries make clear.[29] (The portico of Santa Maria Mater Domini was noted by the authorities as a place of particular iniquity.) In each parish two nobles were appointed to root out the practice and all doctors or barbers called on to treat either man or woman, '*in partem posteriorem confractam per sodomiam*', were obliged by a law of 1467 to report the incident within three days. Retribution was sometimes severe. In the cause of sexual purity more than one poor fellow was burnt to death between the columns of the Piazzetta.

Among other means used to punish unnatural vice was the *cheba*, a sort of cage, primarily intended for delinquent priests, in which the culprit was suspended from the campanile in St Mark's Square. Bread and water could then be let down to him from the bell-chambers. This curious punishment left the condemned man with one unusual expedient that was adopted by a certain Agostino, a priest in the parish of Santa Fosca. Sentenced to the *cheba* in 1518 for gambling and blasphemy, he became the subject of a popular poem in which he expressed his sense of ill-usage, complaining that the urchins on the ground below harassed and ridiculed him with such impudence that to relieve his indignation he was obliged 'to piss on them from above' ('*pissarli adosso*').

At least today's visitors need guard only against the pigeons.

PALAZZO GOZZI

A left turn just beyond the Campo San Cassiano will take us down the Calle della Regina. At the far end of the street, opposite the turning to the Calle de Ca' Bragadin al Cristo, stands no. 2269, the somewhat decrepit palazzo that was the home of Carlo and Gaspar Gozzi. (For a more attractive view of it we can stand on the bridge into the Campo Santa Maria Mater Domini and look at the façade it presents to the square.) In this passage from his memoirs Gozzi describes his return to the house with an army friend after his period of military service:

We reached the entrance, and my companion gazed with wonder at the stately structure of the mansion, which has really all the appearance of a palace. As a connoisseur of architecture, he complimented me upon its fine design. I answered, what indeed he was about to discover by experience, that attractive exteriors sometimes mask discomfort and annoyance. He had plenty of time to admire the façade, while I kept knocking loudly at the housedoor. I might as well have knocked at the portal of a sepulchre. At last a woman, named Eugenia, the guardian-angel of this wilderness, ran to open. To my enquiries she answered, yawning, that the family were in Friuli, but that my brother Gasparo was momently expected. Our luggage had now been brought from the boat, and we began to ascend a handsome marble staircase. No one could have expected that this fine flight of steps would lead to squalor and the haunts of indigence. Yet on surmounting the last stair that was what revealed itself. The stone floors were worn into holes and fissures, which spread in all directions like a cancer. The broken window panes let blasts from every point of the compass play freely to and fro within the draughty chambers. The hangings on the walls were ragged, smirched with smoke and dust, fluttering in tatters. Not a piece remained of that fine gallery of pictures which my grandfather had bequeathed as heirlooms to the family. I only saw some portraits of my ancestors by Titian and Tintoretto still staring from their ancient frames. I gazed at them; they gazed at me; they wore a look of sadness and amazement, as though enquiring how the wealth which they had gathered for their offspring had been dissipated.[30]

FONDACO DEI TURCHI

The Fondaco dei Turchi, overlooking the Grand Canal, is about five minutes from Gozzi's house, along the Calle della Chiesa and the Calle del Tintor, then over the Ponte del Megio. (Notice beside the bridge the yellow house at the corner of the Calle del Spezier. It was here that Marin Sanudo, whose diaries furnish several of the details given in these pages, died in 1536.) The Fondaco only acquired the function of warehouse for Turkish merchants in the seventeenth century. Formerly it was a private residence, where the poet Tasso had stayed in 1562 as a guest of the Duke of Ferrara. Its history from the seventeenth century onwards was one of steady decline, to the point where Ruskin, studying it in the early 1850s, could take it as a symbol of all that was decadent and neglected in modern Venice. His words invest its dilapidation with a kind of splendour. It is, he says, a ghastly ruin. The covering stones have been torn away from it like the shroud from a corpse; its walls are rent into a thousand chasms:

> Soft grass and wandering leafage have rooted themselves in the rents, but they are not suffered to grow in their own wild and gentle way, for the place is in a sort inhabited; rotten partitions are nailed across its corridors, and miserable rooms contrived in its western wing; and here and there the weeds are indolently torn down, leaving their haggard fibres to struggle again into unwholesome growth when the spring next stirs them: and thus, in contest between death and life, the unsightly heap is festering to its fall.[31]

After undergoing one of the nineteenth century's more brutal restoration jobs, it became the home first of the Correr Museum and now of a Natural History Museum which displays among other items a crab of such monstrous size that it might have ambled straight out of a science fiction film. The curious may also see, under the arcade beside the Grand Canal, the sarcophagus of Marin Falier. In 1355 the aged Doge, prompted by senile resentments, became embroiled in a murderous plot to overthrow the State. The nobility of Venice were to be slaughtered in the Piazza and Falier himself proclaimed Prince. In the event, details of the conspiracy were betrayed to the Council of Ten. Falier's sarcophagus tells the rest. When it was opened in the nineteenth century, it revealed the old man's skeleton, with the skull, neatly severed by the headsman's axe, resting between the knees. In the place of his portrait in the Ducal Palace there is just a black curtain inscribed with the words: '*Hic est locus Marini Faledri decapitati pro criminibus.*'

CALLE DEL CAPITELLO TO PONTE BERGAMI

At the far end of the Salizzada which runs past the entrance to the Natural History Museum is the Calle del Capitello. Its towering, lightless walls are forbidding even by Venetian standards, and the name is an indication of at least one murder which took place in this narrow street. *Capitelli* are small shrines, and the lamps which burned before them were the first form of street-lighting that Venice enjoyed. They were placed in the dark corner where murder had been done, partly, as Douglas tells us, that their light should make such secret acts more difficult, partly to awaken kinder thoughts in those who were bent on violence. By the time Felix Fabri visited the city in the late fifteenth century the use of these lights was widespread:

> In every corner, where the ways are twisting and crooked, a lamp is hung, which is lit at night, and lest the light should seem to burn to no purpose, they place against the wall, behind the lamp, an image of the Blessed Virgin, and the lamp burns as much for the honour of the Virgin as for the convenience of wayfarers.[32]

It may well have been the invitation to murder offered by winding alleys and black canals that led the Venetian State to institute general street-lighting as early as the 1730s.

The agreeable streets around this western curve of the Grand Canal have little in the way of monuments to tempt the visitor, but we should at least pass through the distinctive Campo San Giacomo dell'Orio. This is where the hero of L. P. Hartley's *Eustace and Hilda* ends up, as he tries to dash back to Lady Nelly's palazzo on hearing of his sister's illness. When time is short, the pleasant frustrations of finding one's way across Venice can turn to nightmare:

> He looked up. What was this campo with the terra-cotta-washed, round-apsed church, and the trees and the

sweeping crescent of houses that ended in a restaurant covered with a vine? San Giacomo dell'Orio, the street sign told him. He was out of his way, much too far to the left. A panic seized him, an access of train-fever intensified a thousand-fold. He started to run . . .[33]

Before ending our walk opposite the railway station, it is worth pausing a moment at the Ponte Bergami just beyond the church of San Simeone Grande. Look to your left and you will see on the far side of the canal, a short way down, the crumbling façade of the Palazzo Cappello. The palace, for the moment, is derelict, its garden wild and overgrown. A hundred years ago Henry James seems almost to have foreseen their decline when he took this palace for the setting of *The Aspern Papers*:

It was not particularly old, only two or three centuries; and it had an air not so much of decay as of quiet discouragement, as if it had rather missed its career. But its wide front, with a stone balcony from end to end of the *piano nobile* or most important floor, was architectural enough, with the aid of various pilasters and arches; and the stucco with which in the intervals it had long ago been endued was rosy in the April afternoon. It overlooked a clean, melancholy, unfrequented canal, which had a narrow *riva* or convenient footway on either side.[34]

'Our house is very far from the centre,' Miss Bordereau remarks, 'but the little canal is very *comme il faut*.'

The famous garden, which James's narrator busily cultivates to ingratiate himself with Miss Bordereau and her niece, also plays its part in Gabriele d'Annunzio's novel *Il Fuoco*. The scents of fruit and jasmine that permeate the evening air in the garden of the Palazzo Cappello have a peculiar vividness, because the garden itself, 'enclosed like an exiled thing by its girdle of water, becomes all the more intense from its banishment, like the soul of the exile'.[35]

Gardens have a special importance in Venice. In a city whose buildings are everywhere lapped by the sea, there is, as d'Annunzio realized, something both exotic and slightly poignant about the few that have been allowed to survive.

CENTRAL VENICE

0 100 200 300 metres
0 100 200 300 yards

Suggested route
Canals

Ponte di Rialto

GRAND CANAL

Campo S. Bartolomeo
Campo and Church of San Salvatore
Church of San Giuliano
Mercerie
Mercerie
Mercerie
Campo S. Gallo
Calle del Cavalletto
Procuratie Vecchie
Torre dell' Orologio
Piazza San Marco
Calle Vallaresso
Palazzo Giustinian
Campo and Church of San Moisè
C.d. Ridotto
Frezzeria
Calle dei Barcaroli
Ponte dei Barcaroli
Salizzada S. Moisè
Ponte dei Fuseri
Rio del Cavaletto
Calle del Frutariol
Barcaroli
Larga XXII Marzo
C.d. Traghetto
Cal. del Sartor da Veste
Corte Michiel
Campo S. Maria del Giglio
Ramo dei Fuseri
C.d. Teatro
Campo Teatro S. Luca
C.d. Manin
Church of San Luca
Teatro la Fenice
Calle del Forno
R. Terrà o Rio Terrà d. Assassini
Calle Pesaro
Palazzo Benzon
Calle della Mandola
Spezier
Campo Sant' Angelo
Palazzo Morosini
Campo S. Maurizio
Calle del Dose
Museo Fortuny
Piscina S. Samuele
Campiello Nuovo
Church and Campo di S. Stefano
Casetta Rossa
Rio del Orso
Palazzo Barbaro
F. Barbaro
Palazzi Mocenigo
Calle Mocenigo
Calle delle Carrozze
Calle Malipiero
Campo and Church of San Samuele
Campo and Church of San Vitale
Ponte dell' Accademia

3

CENTRAL VENICE

HARRY'S BAR

The area round San Moisè has long been favoured by tourists.
As the vaporetto makes its way across from San Marco to the
Salute and then swings back towards Santa Maria del Giglio,
we can look out at a line of palaces that includes many of the
city's most celebrated hotels – among them the Monaco, the
Europa and Regina, the Bauer Grünwald and the Gritti Palace.
But for the homesick American, returning wearily from
another encounter with the tangled streets beyond the Piazza,
a more welcome sight than any of these is a discreet doorway
in the nearby Calle Vallaresso.

Like St Mark's or the Doge's Palace, Harry's Bar has
become a place of pilgrimage. Frequented by the fictional
characters of writers from Hemingway to Patricia Highsmith,

it has an association with America which, as Gore Vidal explains, goes back to its origins:

> In 1931, an American lamented with his favourite hotel bartender, the late Giuseppe Cipriani, that what Venice lacked was a good bar. The American, whose name was Harry, probably was not the first refugee from American Prohibition to make that observation, although the lengthy Venetian chronicles of two other Americans, Henry James and William Dean Howells, carry no mention of the city's lack of saloons. But Harry was the first to follow the inbred American tradition of wanting to set right a wrong. This was done in the form of financial backing to Cipriani, who found a rope storeroom next to St Mark's *vaporetto* stop and there opened what he called Harry's Bar.
>
> Even without knowing the origin of its history, some American visitors today consider Harry's Bar as being almost extra-territorially *theirs*. Since the closing of the American consulate in the 1970s, it is indeed sometimes the only place for Americans in acute distress to go for comfort and advice. However, Harry's bar was and remains an entirely Venetian operation, though the babble of barbaric voices on summer days and nights is predominantly American. Most important, it is an innovation, perhaps the only one in the ancient city, which has been accepted by the Venetians. It has become one of their own monuments. Like most natives everywhere, they may shy away from actually visiting their monuments (call it the Grant's Tomb or Tower of London syndrome), but they like to know that it is there, and that it is appreciated and frequented by foreign visitors.[1]

FREZZERIA

The other end of the Calle Vallaresso opens into the Salizzada San Moisè almost opposite the Frezzeria. It was at nos 1673–1674 in the Frezzeria, on the corner of the Calle di

Piscina, that Byron took rooms when he arrived in Venice. Above a suitably fashionable clothes shop, the building is beginning, like many in Venice, to look its age; but then the same may well have been true when Byron first saw it in November 1816. He had left England some six months earlier, after his marriage to Annabella Milbanke had ended in separation and scandal. Pursued by evil rumours about his treatment of his wife and his relationship with his half-sister Augusta, he had made first for Geneva and then for Venice. It was here that he settled. A letter to his friend Tom Moore, dated 17 November, explains some of the attractions of the city, and also of this particular house in the Frezzeria:

> It is my intention to remain at Venice during the winter, probably, as it has always been (next to the East) the greenest island of my imagination. It has not disappointed me; though its evident decay would, perhaps, have that effect upon others. But I have been familiar with ruins too long to dislike desolation. Besides, I have fallen in love, which, next to falling into the canal, (which would be of no use, as I can swim) is the best or the worst thing I could do. I have got some extremely good apartments in the house of a 'Merchant of Venice,' who is a good deal occupied with business, and has a wife in her twenty-second year. Marianna (that is her name) is in her appearance altogether like an antelope. She has the large, black, oriental eyes, with that peculiar expression in them which is seen rarely among *Europeans* – even the Italians – and which many of the Turkish women give themselves by tinging the eyelid, – an art not known out of that country, I believe. This expression she has *naturally*, – and something more than this. In short, I cannot describe the effect of this kind of eye – at least upon me.[2]

Marianna was the first, and one of the most enduring of Byron's Venetian loves, and his letters keep up a diverting commentary on the progress of their affair. A couple of months after the letter quoted above, he was writing to Moore again to give an account of a turbulent evening which elsewhere might have ended badly. The letter is revealing in what it tells both of Byron and of Venice:

Now for an adventure. A few days ago a gondolier brought me a billet without a subscription, intimating a wish on the part of the writer to meet me either in gondola or at the island of San Lazaro, or at a third rendezvous indicated in the note. 'I know the country's disposition well' – in Venice 'they do let Heaven see those tricks they dare not show,' &c. &c.; so, for all response, I said that neither of the three places suited me; but that I would either be at home at ten at night *alone*, or at the ridotto at midnight, where the writer might meet me masked. At ten o'clock I was at home and alone (Marianna was gone with her husband to a conversazione), when the door of my apartment opened, and in walked a well-looking and (for an Italian) *bionda* girl of about nineteen, who informed me that she was married to the brother of my *amorosa*, and wished to have some conversation with me. I made a decent reply, and we had some talk in Italian and Romaic (her mother being a Greek of Corfu), when lo! in a very few minutes, in marches, to my very great astonishment, Marianna S, *in propria persona*, and after making polite courtesy to her sister-in-law and to me, without a single word seizes her said sister-in-law by the hair, and bestows upon her some sixteen slaps, which would have made your ear ache only to hear their echo. I need not describe the screaming which ensued. The luckless visitor took flight. I seized Marianna, who, after several vain efforts to get away in pursuit of the enemy, fairly went into fits in my arms; and, in spite of reasoning, eau de Cologne, vinegar, half a pint of water, and God knows what other waters beside, continued so till past midnight.

. . . After about an hour, in comes – who? why, Signor S, her lord and husband, and finds me with his wife fainting upon the sofa, and all the apparatus of confusion, dishevelled hair, hats, handkerchiefs, salts, smelling-bottles – and the lady as pale as ashes without sense or motion. His first question was, 'What is all this?' The lady could not reply – so I did. I told him the explanation was the easiest thing in the world; but in the meantime it would be as well to recover his wife – at least, her senses. This came about in due time of suspiration and respiration.

You need not be alarmed – jealousy is not the order of the day in Venice, and daggers are out of fashion; while duels, on love matters, are unknown – at least, with husbands.[3]

The busy Frezzeria was originally the main centre for shops selling arrows (*frecce*) – an important commodity in a city where, during the fourteenth century, all males between the ages of sixteen and thirty-five were obliged to present themselves for weekly practice with the cross-bow. Returning towards the Salizzada, you might glance down the sottoportico a few yards along on the other side of the street. It leads to the somewhat uninviting Corte del Luganegher, where Casanova lived in 1774.

From the Salizzada a turning to the left takes us down the Calle del Ridotto, at the end of which, on the right, stands the Palazzo Giustinian. It is now the headquarters of the Biennale, but in the nineteenth century, as the Hotel Europa, it was patronized by a range of literary figures, including Gautier, Proust, and de Musset. It was here that George Eliot came with her husband in May 1880, just a month after their marriage. A couple of weeks into their holiday, the bridegroom, John Cross, jumped from the balcony of their room into the Grand Canal and had to be fished out by gondoliers. The episode shook George Eliot and their visit was cut short. Within a few days the unstable Cross had been removed to Verona and thence back to England. In the circumstances it is perhaps not surprising that George Eliot had little of interest to say about the sights of Venice.

RIDOTTO

The Calle del Ridotto takes its name from the famous gambling-house, or *ridotto*, which stood on the other side from

the Palazzo Giustinian, at no. 1361. This was the old Palazzo
Dandolo, just behind what is now the Hotel Monaco. The
State had given permission for Marco Dandolo to open a
public gaming-house in his palace in 1638, but when it was
expanded and embellished in the middle of the following
century, the effects were too devastating to be ignored. Within
twenty years the toll of ruined families had forced the Maggior
Consiglio to take action. On 27 November 1774, 'in order to
stamp out the vice in its principal seat', it decreed the closing of
the Ridotto.

In its heyday the Ridotto was one of the centres of Carnival
Venice, where huge sums were nightly won and lost. Its
appearance in the mid-eighteenth century has been described
by Pompeo Molmenti in his social history of Venice:

> The entrance hall was hung with stamped leather, and
> here the maskers would walk and talk, or would pass
> thence into two little neighbouring chambers with buf-
> fets: at one they sold chocolate, coffee, and tea; at the
> other, wine, cheese, sausages, and fruit. From the en-
> trance hall opened ten large rooms in which the gaming
> tables . . . were set out. At each table sat a nobleman, in
> robe and wig, with piles of sequins and of ducats before
> him ready to hold the bank against all comers provided
> they were either patricians or masked.[4]

One of those who frequented the Ridotto in the last year or
two before it closed was Lorenzo da Ponte, later to become
Mozart's librettist. At the time he was in his early twenties and
in love with a woman whose brother was a furious gambler. A
striking episode in his memoirs begins with a typical scene at
one of the gaming tables. The brother has taken da Ponte's
own recent winnings, promising to double them:

> It was already past midnight, and all the other bankers had
> put down the cards. But play began again now for
> desperate stakes. In the first two games his luck was
> wonderfully good. He soon had a little mountain of gold
> in front of him. I sat on one side of him and his sister on
> the other. We did not dare speak, but we made signs to

him with our eyes and hands and feet to make him stop playing. But all was in vain. He began a third game but did not finish it: about half way through all his money was gone. With wonderful coolness he then put down the cards, 'looked at me with a mocking laugh and a toss of the head,' and taking his sister by the hand, bade me good-night and went away.

I need not say what my feelings were. I withdrew into the 'chamber of sighs,' a room so called because it was frequented by unfortunate lovers or gamblers, for talk or sighing or sleep. After some time I fell asleep and did not wake till broad daylight, when all the company had gone, except a few who, like myself, had slept there.

A man in a mask sitting near me, seeing me awake, begged a couple of *soldi* of me. After having felt in my pockets in vain, I put my hand into the fob of my coat, and what was my surprise and joy to find some sequins there, which, as they were underneath a handkerchief, had not been noticed and so had not been taken out of my pockets with the rest of the money when my mistress's brother arrived home. It was only with difficulty that I concealed my joyful surprise. However, having no other change, I offered my neighbour one of the sequins. At first he refused to take it, but afterwards, looking hard at me, said, 'I will take it only on condition that you allow me to return it to you in my own house.' So saying, he took a playing card and on the back wrote the name of the street and the number of his house, saying as he gave it to me that he was sure I should not regret paying him a visit. But just then I was thinking only of my mistress and the fact that some of the money was saved, so I put the card into my pocket without paying attention to it and hurried home at once.[5]

It is some time later, on the first Sunday in Lent, that da Ponte comes across the card again and is driven by curiosity to visit the address. The masked man from the Ridotto turns out to be a native of Leghorn whom hardship had forced to the life of a professional beggar. In a curious scene, which da Ponte insists is a truthful record of events, the old man reveals how well he has prospered over the years and shows the bemused visitor his horde of money. To da Ponte's astonishment the details of his life are already well known to the man, who has displayed his wealth for a purpose:

> 'There are five thousand *zecchini* there, and I will give them to you the day you marry my daughter. Afterwards at my death, or before if you need it, you will have another four thousand, which is all I possess, but you must promise me always to remember the poor, and that I believe you will do. I have had you in my eye for about two years. I liked your appearance immediately I saw you. For some years I sat begging at the foot of the Ponte San Gregorio where you passed by every day, and your repeated acts of charity to me there won my good-will and respect for you. It always seemed marvellous to me that you should give me alms for I knew the state you were in, and it made me feel that you must have a kindly-disposed heart, and that, I think, is the sum of all the virtues and the soul of true religion.'[6]

Obsessed by his current mistress, who later does what she can to get him killed, da Ponte refuses the old man's offer and after a pleasant day with him and his daughter leaves the house. Within a few months the daughter marries someone else and da Ponte is left with his regrets.

In any other city it would be impossible to take the story for more than a fairy-tale, but eighteenth-century Venice is itself so close to fairy-tale that what would elsewhere be the stuff of fantasy seems almost the texture of daily life. Perhaps the future librettist of *Don Giovanni* and *Così Fan Tutte* really did pause from time to time as he crossed the Ponte San Gregorio to drop a coin into this unlikely beggar's hand.

CHURCH OF SAN MOISÈ

So absorbingly ugly is the modern façade of the Hotel Bauer Grünwald that if one enters the Campo San Moisè from the

Piazza, the church can almost escape notice. Only the defiant have had anything very charitable to say about San Moisè since Ruskin passed judgement: 'one of the basest examples of the basest school of the Renaissance', was his characteristically firm assessment. The wilder flights of the baroque are not always a happy sight, but one can feel a certain sympathy with the hero of L. P. Hartley's *Eustace and Hilda* in his hesitant refusal to be intimidated by the art historians:

> Not for the first time the crumbling, florid front of the church of San Moisè claimed his attention. Ruskin had loaded it with obloquy: in his eyes it was frivolous, ignoble, immoral. Eustace was determined to like it: half one's pleasure in Venice was lost if one could not stomach the rococo and the baroque. But this evening, as he stood on the little bridge and watched the pigeons strutting to and fro, hardly visible among the swags, cornucopias, and swing-boat forms whose lateral movement seemed to rock the church from side to side, his interest was not in the morality or otherwise of the tormented stonework, but in the state of mind of people to whom such exuberance of spirit was as natural as the air they breathed. Never a hint, in all that aggregation of masonry, of diffidence or despondency, no suggestion of a sad, tired mind finding its only expression in a stretch of blank wall.[7]

Less anxiously, Sean O'Faolain observes the life of the campo on an August day in 1948:

> This torrid morning I am passing out of the dimness of San Moisè, idly wondering if it was the Oriental influence that sanctified Moses as I look back again at the carnal clusters on the façade that threw Ruskin into such a spluttering rage. I lean over a humped bridge beneath whose shade a gondolier lies fast asleep in his gondola. I pass on and pause beside an entirely modern chemist's window, packed with nostrums, glittering with feminine war-tackle. Then I stroll a few feet beyond and come on one of those eloquent obituaries that Italian piety pastes

on dead walls, or hangs in shop-windows, or inserts in
the newspapers to show the world that dead friends are
not forgotten . . . As I read this pious memorial, behind
me are the chaffering black-marketeers, offering tobacco,
scents, foreign money. The crowds float past unheeding.
I can just see the feet of the sleeping gondolier, sticking
out into the sun that burns his soles. In the flickering
miasma of the heat the statues on the church seem to
sway.[8]

SPIES IN SAN MOISÈ

In the days of the Republic a bystander might occasionally
have seen furtive passers-by pausing a few yards from the
church's extravagant façade to slip a note into the *bocca di leone*
of San Moisè, the lion's mouth which acted as a post-box for
secret denunciations. It was here that in May 1779 an unknown
hand posted the denunciation which drove da Ponte from the
city.[9] In his case the accusations of various kinds of sexual and
financial misconduct were probably well justified, but in spite
of safeguards, the system was open to abuse, and it engendered
widespread fear. An eighteenth-century satirical work, in
which Casanova probably had a hand, makes the point with
some bitterness: 'A foreigner who travels to this Republic
should leave his tongue at Fusina and arrive in Venice mute.
Silence is the emblem of this government: everything is secret
and cloaked in mystery. Political doings are covered by a thick
veil of darkness. In Venice those who talk are buried alive in a
tomb covered with lead.'[10]

As this implies, the State's concern was primarily political.
Its attitude is summed up by Charles de Brosses, President of
the Burgundian Parliament, writing in 1739: 'I will tell you
that nowhere on earth do liberty and licence have a more
complete empire than in Venice. Stay clear of politics and for
the rest do what you will.'[11]

Whether true or not, the story of how Lord Chesterfield
unsettled the philosophical calm of Montesquieu conveys
something of the atmosphere of the time. The Frenchman had

merely been taking in the sights and trying to make a study of Venetian laws. On a whim, Chesterfield gave him to understand that he had come under the eye of the State Inquisitors. The effect on Montesquieu was dramatic: he burned his notes, packed his bags, and headed for Holland.

Historians have long been sceptical about the myths that lie behind this sort of story, but it is nonetheless true that spying was something of a Venetian speciality. It was the province of the so-called Council of Ten, which had been established in the wake of Baiamonte Tiepolo's conspiracy and from which the three State Inquisitors were drawn. The ten Senators who made up this Tribunal were elected annually from the larger Maggior Consiglio. Acting in concert with the Doge, they exercised wide executive powers, and from the start they had developed a brilliant intelligence network, both inside the city and out. By the eighteenth century its scope had been much reduced, but even so, those luckless figures who came to the attention of the Ten were likely to be scrutinized down to the smallest details of their daily lives. We know, for example, that on 30 June 1791 a patrician named Pietro Giacomo Foscarini passed close to the spot where we are now standing on his way to visit a tailor. The report was made out by a certain Gerolamo Mazzucato who had dogged his footsteps throughout the day. When Foscarini emerged from his house, he went first to the Della Nave, a café in the Calle Larga San Marco:

Ordered a coffee. Stayed half an hour or so, but spoke to no one. Went to the Vecchie Procuratie, to the snuff-merchants, for an ounce of snuff. Walked in the Mercerie for perhaps fifteen minutes, and then home. About one o'clock came out again; to the Delle Rive, the café under the Padaglione. There till two, spoke to no one. Then to the tailor on the San Moisè bridge, and spent half an hour talking to the owner. Owner and he came out together and proceeded to the Piazza, where they strolled until nearly three, talking. Parted. The Noble Gentleman went to the Della Nave and met some people there. Said little, drank a barley-water and left at four-thirty. Back to the

Piazza, walked under the Vecchie Procuratie and greeted someone I did not recognize. Went to the Arco Celeste, said very little and nobody addressed him. Strolled once more until five o'clock or so; back home.[12]

If this was an average summer's day, the Ten probably had good reason to fear that men's minds might turn to intrigue.

LODGINGS IN SAN MOISÈ

To leave the Campo San Moisè we cross the bridge into the Calle Larga over what Corvo described as 'that dreadful little ditch of a canal by Sanmoise which is lined on both sides with the gondole of the most disagreeable extortionate nasty-tempered gondolieri in Venice'. A writer who remembered the area more kindly was Théophile Gautier. For him San Moisè was *'le coin où nous avons passé un mois si heureux'*. After an initial stay at the Hotel Europa, he took lodgings just beside the canal in rooms recently vacated by a Russian prince. Not, he adds, that the word prince should mislead people: 'In Venice one can treat oneself to the luxury of a palace at friendly prices. A jewel from the hand of Sansovino or Scamozzi is cheaper to rent than a garret in the Rue de la Paix, and our lodging was part of a simple house with pink rendering, like most of the houses in Venice.'[13] His only complaint was one shared by the majority of travellers to Venice before the twentieth century:

> The great business before going to bed is the hunt for insects, vicious mosquitoes that particularly torment foreigners, on whom they hurl themselves with the sensual appetite of a gourmet savouring some rare and exotic dish. The grocery shops and pharmacies sell a fumigating powder which you burn on a small stove with all the windows closed, and which sees off or suffocates the terrible insects. This powder seems to be more obnoxious to people than to mosquitoes, and the number of bumps on our hands and face each morning were an indication of how ineffective it was as a remedy. The

most sensible course is not to put any light near the bed and to seal yourself hermetically inside the veils of the mosquito net.[14]

Gautier's experience might make one doubtful of the claims of local pharmacists, but the *Cook's Handbook* for 1875 helpfully lists an 'English chemist', albeit with a rather un-English name: 'Dr Zampironi, S. Moisè, near Piazza S. Marco. Prescriptions carefully prepared – patent medicines – special pastilles for killing mosquitoes.'

HOTEL REGINA

A few yards along the Calle Larga XXII Marzo, on the other side of Corvo's 'dreadful little ditch', the Calle del Traghetto leads down to the Grand Canal almost exactly opposite the Salute. At the end, a convenient jetty enables one to walk out and survey the Hotel Regina, formerly the Casa Alvisi, home of Katharine de Kay Bronson. Originally from New York, Mrs Bronson became known in Venice for her hospitality to a long succession of English and American visitors. In the 1880s she provided a base for both Browning and Henry James, lodging them in the Palazzo Giustiniani-Recanati, just behind the Casa Alvisi. As Mrs Prest in *The Aspern Papers*, it is she who shepherds the narrator through the canals and brings him to the house of Miss Bordereau and her niece. Earlier, James had paid a pleasant tribute to life at the Casa Alvisi in the closing lines of his best known essay on Venice:

> If you are happy you will find yourself, after a June day in Venice (about ten o'clock), on a balcony that overhangs the Grand Canal, with your elbows on the broad ledge, a cigarette in your teeth and a little good company beside you. The gondolas pass beneath, the watery surface gleams here and there from their lamps, some of which are coloured lanterns that move mysteriously in the darkness . . .[15]

LA FENICE

Back on the Calle Larga, we are at a convenient point from
which to turn aside for a look at the Fenice, just a short walk
along the Calle del Sartor da Veste. It was not one of Venice's
earliest theatres, but since it opened in 1791 it has always
been the most celebrated, scene of the opening nights of
both *Rigoletto* and *La Traviata* as well as, more recently,
Stravinsky's *The Rake's Progress*.

At the heart of the city the Fenice has a symbolic importance
that outweighs its actual function, for it is an elaborate shrine
to one of Venice's most striking characteristics. For centuries
the rulers of this theatrical city, cheerfully aided by the people,
made calculated use of its dramatic possibilities. In 1177 they
staged the great reconciliation scene between Frederick Bar-
barossa and Pope Alexander III, when the Emperor knelt to
the Pope in the vestibule of St Mark's, and thereafter the
diplomatic advantages to be gained from putting on an im-
pressive show were rarely missed. Now that Venice has
grown old, it is easy for us to see in its handsome, flaking
façades the elegiac appeal of an abandoned stage-set. Or
perhaps, as Henry James suggests in *The Aspern Papers*, the
theatre has merely taken on a more domestic tone. The city, he
says, is like an immense collective apartment, furnished with
palaces and churches:

> And somehow the splendid common domicile, familiar,
> domestic and resonant, also resembles a theatre, with
> actors clicking over bridges and, in straggling pro-
> cessions, tripping along fondamentas. As you sit in your
> gondola the footways that in certain parts edge the canals
> assume to the eye the importance of a stage, meeting it at
> the same angle, and the Venetian figures, moving to and
> fro against the battered scenery of their little houses of
> comedy, strike you as members of an endless dramatic
> troupe.[16]

By the time Ruskin and his bride visited the Fenice, it had
acquired a genuine right to the name of Phoenix, having been
destroyed by fire in 1836 and rebuilt shortly afterwards. It had

also by then become a focus for protests against the Austrian occupation. Not that this was of great concern to Effie Ruskin, who found the manners and dress of the Austrian officers beyond reproach. Even for her, however, the social demands of an evening at the Fenice could be oppressive. She went there for Rossini's opera *Semiramide* two days after Christmas, 1851:

> We came away before the end as it was so long. I wish they did not talk so much in the Theatre for it is impossible to pay any attention to the Opera, for first came Nugent talking English as fast as he could, at the same time the Princess talking her Venetian and General Duodo replying – then came Falkenhayn with his German & Wrbna with his French making your box a sort of Babel, and as it would be considered quite contrary to etiquette that Ladies should ever be left alone in their box, whenever one gentleman has paid his visit of a quarter of an hour or so another arrives to take his place and you never have a chance of being alone a minute. I complained of it last night to Mdme. Pal. and they were all against me; they said that the Theatre was public property and every body had a right to call upon any body that they knew, and as most people went every night for an hour it was economical as it saved them lighting their rooms at home, and that having a box at the Opera was the cheapest way for all to see people & society.[17]

PONTE DEI BARCAROLI

Before returning to the Calle Larga, devotees of George Sand might like to walk a few yards down the Calle del Frutariol as far as the pretty bridge that crosses the Rio dei Barcaroli. Writing the Preface to a new edition of *André* in 1851, Sand recalled: 'It was in Venice that I dreamed up and wrote this novel. I was living in a little low house alongside a narrow strip of water which was green and yet limpid, close to the Ponte dei Barcarolli . . .'[18] She could not have asked for a more exquisitely Venetian setting. It was here that she had come in the spring of 1834 with Pietro Pagello, the young doctor whose appearance on the scene had put an end to her tortured relationship with Alfred de Musset. The 'little low house' was the Ca' Mezzani, now no. 1880 in the Corte Minelli, which the couple shared with Pagello's brother and stepsister. Glimpses of this ménage, sketched with ironic affection, can be found in Sand's *Lettres d'un voyageur*, the first three of which she wrote while she was living here.

Corte Michiel

Just before the Calle Larga veers round to the left, a street beside the consulate of Monaco leads off in the other direction to the secluded little Corte Michiel, where Countess Isabella Teotocchi Albrizzi lived. It was on a visit to her house, one of the great literary salons of the time, that Byron first made the acquaintance of the nineteen-year-old Countess Teresa Guiccioli. The Countess's recent marriage was not of a kind to inconvenience her social life, and when she met Byron again the following year, she was happy to accept him as her *cavalier servente*. This genial institution available to married women of the day cast the man in the role of courtier, attendant, general dogsbody and, if he was lucky, lover. English writers tended to take a dim view of it. Samuel Sharp, travelling to Venice in the previous century, had commented:

> Gallantry is so epidemical in this city, that few of the Ladies escape the contagion. No woman can go into a public place, but in the company of a Gentleman, called here, a *Cavaliere Servente*, and in other parts of *Italy*, a *Cicesbeo*. This Cavaliere is always the same person; and she not only is attached to him, but to him singly; for no other woman joins the company, but it is usual for them to sit alone in the box, at the opera, or play-house, where they must be, in a manner, by themselves, as the theatres are so very dark that the spectators can hardly be said to be in company with one another. . . . On the other hand, the husband has his revenge; for he never fails to be the *Cavaliere Servente* of some other woman; and, I am told, it would be so ridiculous for a husband to appear in publick

with his wife, that there is no instance of such a phe-
nomenon; and, therefore, it is impossible for a woman to
bear up against the torrent of this fashion.[19]

Given its various constraints, it is a somewhat startling role for
Byron to have accepted. As he wrote to his friend Hobhouse:

> I like women – God he knows – but the more their sys-
> tem here developes upon me – the worse it seems – after
> Turkey too – here the *polygamy* is all on the female
> side. – I have been an intriguer, a husband, and now I am
> a Cavalier Servente. – by the holy! – it is a strange
> sensation.[20]

The account of it he gives in *Beppo* conveys even less
enthusiasm:

> But 'Cavalier Servente' is the phrase
>   Used in the politest circles to express
> This supernumerary slave, who stays
>   Close to the lady as a part of dress,
> Her word the only law which he obeys.
>   His is no sinecure, as you may guess;
> Coach, servants, gondola, he goes to call,
>   And carries fan and tippet, gloves and shawl.

But in spite of occasional backsliding, Byron seems to have
taken to the job readily enough. In something close to respect-
ability he and his mistress settled down to grow plump
together in Ravenná, until domestic and political upheavals
drove them first to Pisa and then to Genoa. It was perhaps
surprising – not least to Byron himself – that the relationship
was still unbroken when the affairs of Greece called him away
to his death.

CAMPO SANTA MARIA DEL GIGLIO

At the end of the Calle Larga a small bridge crosses the canal,
and then the Calle delle Ostreghe takes us into the Campo
Santa Maria del Giglio. For those who travel in comfort this is

a square of blessed memory, since it houses the Gritti Palace hotel, whose guests in recent years have included Hemingway, Graham Greene, and Somerset Maugham. It is here that Hemingway's Colonel Cantwell stays in *Across the River and into the Trees* – as the author himself had done while writing the book.

Before it became a modern hotel the Gritti provided lodgings for Ruskin and Effie during their visit to Venice in 1851–2, when Ruskin wrote the second volume of *The Stones of Venice*. His letters in the early days of their tenancy show a certain anxiety to stress the diligent, respectable, and economical nature of their life, probably because when the idea of looking for a place of their own was first mooted the response of Ruskin's father had been a masterpiece of Victorian foreboding:

> . . . would it either morally or religiously harmonize with your feelings or strengthen your minds or Character? . . . Mama deems it a duty to beseech of you to pause before you plunge too far into the fascinations of Continental Life – They never yet I fancy did much good to either man or woman – Woman especially . . . I cannot at once say I entirely approve of hiring House or Palace abroad yet – It sounds Byronish or Shelleyish . . . how few of our best men have dwelt in Foreign Land? – Gibbon is the most known after Byron & neither would we like you to resemble . . .[21]

In spite of the vistas of expatriate debauchery which suggested themselves to Ruskin père, the couple went ahead and secured a comfortable suite of rooms at the Gritti (then called the Casa Wetzlar after its current owner), where they stayed for some eight months. It might have added a certain piquancy to their defiance of parental fears to know how close the palace had come to being the scene of Byron's excesses. He had bargained for it before moving to the Palazzo Mocenigo but was unable to agree terms with the owner.

At the other end of the square from the Gritti – and one more source of dismay to Ruskin – stands the church of Santa Maria del Giglio, built in the late seventeenth century. Quite without religious significance, its confidently pagan façade stands as a monument to the man who paid for it, Antonio Barbaro. His statue, looking suitably imperial, dominates the centre, while on the left Fame trumpets his deeds towards the square. The rest is given over to allegorical virtues, statues of his relations, and flattering memorials of his rather inglorious military career.

Serious tourists might prefer to be spared the sort of episodes that Marin Sanudo liked to record in his diary, but for the more frivolous they are an engaging aspect of the city's life. Venetian youth were reckoned to be among the most unruly in Italy and the hapless boy who met his end here on 24 January 1518 must have been one of a familiar breed:

> It happened that a madcap youth, dressed as an old man, had a sort of cage with a phallus inside, which he went around showing to the women; but it seems that at Santa Maria del Giglio, when he showed it to a young woman at a certain balcony there, someone who had an interest in her came out, stabbed him with a dagger and killed him. He was 16 years old.[22]

CALLE DEL DOSE

A couple of attractive bridges away, continuing in the direction of the Accademia, is the Campo San Maurizio. At no. 2760, on the corner of the Calle del Piovan, we pass the imposing Palazzo Bellavite, which was the home in the eighteenth century of the vernacular poet Giorgio Baffo and also, for the winter of 1803–4, of Alessandro Manzoni, author of *I Promessi Sposi*. It was in fact the house of Manzoni's uncle, to whom the eighteen-year-old had been sent on a visit, probably to cure him of an unfortunate liaison in his native Milan. He stayed just long enough to pick up a venereal infection and become a habitué of the salon of the Countess Benzon (see p. 94), though there is no suggestion that the two achievements were related. In old age, Manzoni looked back on his winter in Venice with pleasure. He is said to have talked of the city to one Venetian lady with such vividness that she asked if he had been there recently. 'About sixty-seven years ago,' was the reply.[23]

From the left-hand side of the campo it is worth following the Calle del Dose down to the Grand Canal for the view it offers of the far bank, across to the low white stones of the Guggenheim Museum and the beautiful façade of the Palazzo Dario. Just to the left of this vantage point is the little Casetta Rossa, where Canova had his studio. Later it was the headquarters of Gabriele d'Annunzio, who lived here during the First World War. Invisible from the fondamenta, it can be reached via an alley off the Calle del Dose; but the best view, as usual, is from the Grand Canal. Hemingway's Colonel takes it in on his way to the Gritti, accompanied by his army driver:

'Jackson,' he said, 'that small villa on the left belonged to Gabriele d'Annunzio, who was a great writer.'

'Yes, sir,' said Jackson, 'I'm glad to know about him. I never heard of him.'

'I'll check you out on what he wrote if you ever want to read him,' the Colonel said. 'There are some fair English translations.'

'Thank you, sir,' said Jackson. 'I'd like to read him any time I have time. He has a nice practical looking place. What did you say the name was?'

'D'Annunzio,' the Colonel said. 'Writer.'

He added to himself, not wishing to confuse Jackson, nor be difficult, as he had been with the man several times that day, writer, poet, national hero, phraser of the dialectic of Fascism, macabre egotist, aviator, commander, or rider, in the first of the fast torpedo attack boats, Lieutenant-Colonel of Infantry without knowing how to command a company, nor a platoon properly, the great, lovely writer of *Notturno* whom we respect, and jerk.[24]

CALLE DEL SPEZIER

The street which leads from the Campo San Maurizio to the Campo San Stefano is one of a number in Venice called the Calle del Spezier. The name indicates that it was a street of *spezieri* or pharmacists. In ancient Venice pharmacy was a highly regarded craft whose practitioners had, among other privileges, the right to marry a Venetian noblewoman. From the Middle Ages the city was famous for its *triaca*, sometimes rather misleadingly translated as treacle. This was a concoction of aromatic herbs, amber, and other ingredients imported from the East, which was reckoned to be a cure for more or less anything. There was consternation when it failed to cope with the plague in the fourteenth century, but in spite of this its reputation continued to grow. In 1646 John Evelyn made sure to pack some along with his books, pictures, and Murano glass, before returning to England, and in our own times both H. V. Morton and James Morris have managed to purchase some from what must now be a greatly depleted stock.

The ceremony of preparing *triaca*, which Evelyn had gone to the trouble of observing, 'for tis extremely pompous & worth seeing', took place at specific times of the year. The drugs to be powdered were placed in a mortar outside the pharmacy, where men in a special costume and chanting a special refrain carried out the pounding. The Calle del Spezier still opens into the Campo San Stefano just beside a pharmacy, and in front of it can be seen a number of hollowed paving stones in which the bronze mortars were set.

CAMPO SAN STEFANO: PALAZZO BARBARO

In earlier times the pharmacy on this corner of the spacious Campo San Stefano must have enjoyed a particularly lucrative trade. Like San Polo, the square was much used for public entertainments. It was here that the last Venetian bull-fight took place in 1802. A disaster in which one of the stands in front of the Palazzo Morosini collapsed, killing a number of spectators, hastened the end of the sport in Venice. As at San

Polo, this aspect of Venetian life was not always welcome to
the clergy. On the church at the far end of the square another of
the plaques prohibiting games can still be seen.

The church itself is a handsome Gothic building which
invites a visit. 'For sheer comfort and pleasure,' writes E. V.
Lucas, 'I think that S. Stefano is the first church in Venice.' The
burial place of the eighteenth-century composer Giovanni
Gabrieli, it is a church that was once more notable for acts of
desecration than of piety. Tassini tells us that between 1348
and 1594 it had to be reconsecrated six times because blood had
been shed on its stones.

At the other end of the square the main thoroughfare takes
us past the church of San Vitale to the Accademia bridge. But
first walk down the little fondamenta to the left, which leads to
the edge of the Palazzo Barbaro. A bell beside the door has the
name Curtis inscribed on a stone inset. This is the family who
have owned the palace since 1885. Amongst those who enjoyed their hospitality in the early years was Henry James. It
was in the summer of 1887 that he first came here, in the course
of an extended Italian tour following the publication of *The
Princess Casamassima*. Fond as he was of Mrs Bronson, the
accommodation she offered in the Palazzo Giustiniani-
Recanati, where he had stayed earlier in the year, was not
really to his taste. He felt that the damp winter air had
combined with the 'insalubrious' apartment to give him an
attack of jaundice, and he was grateful, when he came back
in May, for the more lavish appointments of the Palazzo
Barbaro. Later the kindness of the Curtis family was returned
when their home became the Palazzo Leporelli in *The Wings of
the Dove*. It was exactly what the dying heroine required:

> 'no dreadful, no vulgar hotel; but if it can at all be
> managed – you know what I mean – some fine old rooms,
> wholly independent, for a series of months. Plenty of
> them, too, and the more interesting the better: part of a
> palace, historic and picturesque, but strictly inodorous,
> where we shall be to ourselves, with a cook, don't you
> know? – with servants, frescoes, tapestries, antiquities,
> the thorough make-believe of a settlement.'[25]

Here, 'with the fine old faded palaces opposite and the slow Adriatic tide beneath', Milly Theale lives out the final weeks of her life. Sketching only the lightest details, as in the scene where Milly receives one of her suitors in the *sala*, James manages to suggest the outlines, clear and yet mysterious, of the classic Venetian fantasy: 'The casements between the arches were open, the ledge of the balcony broad, the sweep of the canal, so overhung, admirable, and the flutter towards them of the loose white curtain an invitation to she scarce knew what.'[26]

Looking back from the Accademia bridge, we have a fine view of the palace, just to the right of the Rio del'Orso – more delicate than its neighbour, crumbling a little above the water, with a charming balcony and round marble insets in red and green above the window arches.

CALLE MALIPIERO

Instead of walking back through the Campo San Stefano, we can turn left immediately after the church of San Vitale and carry on until we pass under the sagging beams of the house across the end of the calle. Just beyond is the Calle Malipiero, a narrow street with windows heavily barred on the ground floor and shuttered above. On the lower stretches of the wall the plaster has flaked off to reveal the usual decomposing brickwork. Half-way down, there is a solitary shop that specializes in carnival masks – a lingering echo of the eighteenth-century world described by the modern historian and art critic Marcel Brion:

> The carnival opened, in fact, on the first Sunday in October and went on until Lent, with a short interval from Christmas Day till Epiphany. In other words, for six months every year the people abandoned their regular avocations, and, protected by the anonymity of the mask, threw themselves into the lighthearted pastimes which immediately became their main pre-occupation. . . .

The mask most usually worn by ladies and gentlemen of rank was an extraordinary white face, adorned with a huge nose shaped like the beak of a bird of prey, through which the wearer breathed. When we come across the mask today in museums or collections of old customs, there seems to be something disconcerting, frightening, almost ghostly about it. For the 18th-century Venetians, however, it had the advantage of covering the face completely. Furthermore, it was always worn with a long black cloak which hid the entire body.[27]

That a carnival shop should survive here in the Calle Malipiero seems entirely appropriate when we read the plaque at the end of the street: it was in this calle that Giacomo Casanova was born on 2 April 1725. The church of San Samuele, which we have just reached, was where he was baptized.

PALAZZO MOCENIGO

The district of San Samuele has more than its share of Venetian dead ends, some of them marvellously perverse, but if we leave the campo by the Calle delle Carrozze, with the campanile on our right, we can walk in a more or less straight line for about a hundred and fifty yards until we pass the Calle Mocenigo. At the end of this street are the four Palazzi Mocenigo, which can best be seen by standing at the vaporetto stop of San Tomà and looking across from the other side of the Grand Canal.

Of the four palaces the first (nearest St Mark's) was the one in which the philosopher Giordano Bruno was staying when he was arrested by agents of the Inquisition. He had come to Venice in the autumn of 1591 at the request of Giovanni Mocenigo, who wanted the sage to teach him 'the art of memory and invention'. At a time when religious orthodoxy was enforced by the rack, Bruno's journey to Italy was an act of extraordinary foolhardiness. Mocenigo gave him hospitality, listened to his teachings, and then betrayed him – constrained, he said, by a pious conscience and the urgings of his confessor. On the night of 22 May 1592 Bruno was taken from his bed and locked in a room of the palace until the following evening, when Mocenigo handed him over to the officers of the Inquisition. It took a long time to arrange his death. After eight years of imprisonment and cross-examination, he was finally consigned to the flames in the Campo de' Fiori in Rome on 17 February 1600.

The most imposing of the Mocenigo palaces is the third in line as one moves down the Grand Canal towards the station. Between the two windows on the right of the entrance a plaque records Lord Byron's residence here from 1818–19. The chaotic household in which he managed to write the first two cantos of *Don Juan* was the subject of numerous pages of contemporary gossip, and scenes from this period of his life have continued to mould our image of him: the restless, romantic figure staving off boredom with a string of mistresses, riding on the Lido, swimming the length of the Grand Canal, talking till dawn in the company of Shelley, prowling through the vast rooms of a palace inhabited by a shifting population of servants, acquaintances, hangers-on, and half-tamed animals. The author of *Childe Harold* was fast expending his youth. In an uncharitable moment Shelley wrote home to the novelist Thomas Love Peacock:

> The fact is, that first, the Italian women are perhaps the most contemptible of all who exist under the moon; the most ignorant, the most disgusting, the most bigotted, the most filthy. Countesses smell so of garlick that an ordinary Englishman cannot approach them. Well, L[ord] B[yron] is familiar with the lowest sort of these women, the people his gondolieri pick up in the streets. He allows fathers & mothers to bargain with him for their daughters, & though this is common enough in Italy, yet for an Englishman to encourage such sickening vice is a melancholy thing. He associates with wretches who seem almost to have lost the gait & phisiognomy of man, & who do not scruple to avow practices which are not only not named but I believe seldom even conceived in England. He says he disapproves, but he endures. [28]

The dominating presence of these years, apart from the poet himself, is that of the baker's wife Margharita Cogni, La Fornarina. She was tall and dark, with fine black eyes, 'a thorough Venetian in her dialect – in her thoughts – in her countenance – in every thing'.

Byron had met her in the summer of 1817 as he rode one evening along the banks of the Brenta. They soon came to an agreement:

> She said that she had no objection to make love with me – as she was married – and all married women did it – but that her husband (a baker) was somewhat ferocious – and would do her a mischief. – In short – in a few evenings we arranged our affairs – and for two years – in the course of which I had more women than I can count or recount – she was the only one who preserved over me an ascendancy – which was often disputed & never impaired. – As she herself used to say publicly – 'It don't matter – he may have five hundred – but he will always come back to me'.[29]

Of all the stories of La Fornarina's passion and violence, the most striking is Byron's image of her stormswept figure on the steps outside the Palazzo Mocenigo:

> In the autumn one day going to the Lido with my Gondoliers – we were overtaken by a heavy squall and the Gondola put in peril – hats blown away – boat filling – oar lost – tumbling sea – thunder – rain in torrents – night coming – & wind increasing. – On our return – after a tight struggle: I found her on the open steps of the Mocenigo palace on the Grand Canal – with her great black eyes flashing through her tears and the long dark hair which was streaming drenched with rain over her brows & breast; – she was perfectly exposed to the storm – and the wind blowing her hair & dress about her tall thin figure – and the lightning flashing round her – with the waves rolling at her feet – made her look like Medea alighted from her chariot – or the Sybil of the tempest that was rolling around her – the only living thing within hail

at that moment except ourselves. – On seeing me safe –
she did not wait to greet me as might be expected – but
calling out to me – 'Ah! Can' della Madonna xe esto il
tempo per andar' al Lido?' (ah! Dog of the Virgin! – is this
a time to go to Lido?) ran into the house – and solaced
herself with scolding the boatmen for not foreseeing the
'temporale'. – I was told by the servants that she had only
been prevented from coming in a boat to look after me –
by the refusal of all the Gondoliers of the Canal to put out
into the harbour in such a moment and that then she sate
down on the steps in all the thickest of the Squall – and
would neither be removed nor comforted. Her joy at
seeing me again – was moderately mixed with ferocity –
and gave me the idea of a tigress over her recovered
Cubs.[30]

Although Byron is the only British resident honoured with
a plaque, he was by no means the first to be associated with the
Palazzo Mocenigo, which had been the home in the early
seventeenth century of the formidable Alathea Talbot, Countess of Arundel. A hundred years later the palace was occupied
by another Englishwoman of similarly forceful character.
Lady Mary Wortley Montagu had come to Venice in the
summer of 1739. Famous as a traveller and an intellectual, she
was also famous, less happily, as the butt of some of Alexander
Pope's most vitriolic satire. Amicably separated from her
diplomat husband, she found in Venice an atmosphere of
tolerance which encouraged her to make it her home for two
extended periods over the next twenty years. The one perma-
nent vexation was the stream of brainless and boorish English
youths descending on Venice in the course of their Grand
Tour:

Here are inundations of them broke in upon us this
carnival, and my apartment must be their refuge, the
greater part of them having kept an inviolable fidelity to
the languages their nurses taught them. Their whole
business abroad (as far as I can perceive) being to buy new
cloaths, in which they shine in some obscure coffeehouse, where they are sure of meeting only one another;

and after the important conquest of some waiting gentle-
woman of an opera Queen, who perhaps they remember
as long as they live, return to England excellent judges of
men and manners.[31]

CAMPO SANT' ANGELO

From the Calle Mocenigo we can make our way via the Piscina
San Samuele and the Campiello dei Morti (now tactfully
renamed Campiello Nuovo) to the Campo Sant'Angelo.
Lined with handsome palaces, the square is distinguished by
two well-heads, in one of which a widow's corpse was
discovered in the summer of 1716. Although it lies midway
between the Accademia and the Rialto, the Campo Sant'-
Angelo often seems curiously empty by comparison with
other large squares on the main city routes. It has few shops
and no large cafés. Especially at night, one's footsteps seem to
send back a lonelier echo than usual. The camp is not well lit
and the outline of the listing campanile of San Stefano makes a
strange presence behind the buildings of the square. It is a place
easy to people with figures from the past. In his early twenties,
when he was making a precarious living as a professional
musician, Casanova fell in with one of the rowdy gangs for
which Venice was famed:

> We often spent our nights roaming through different
> quarters of the city, thinking up the most scandalous
> practical jokes and putting them into execution. We
> amused ourselves by untying the gondolas moored be-
> fore private houses, which then drifted with the current to
> one side of the Grand Canal or the other, and making
> merry over the curses the gondoliers would call down
> on us the next morning when they did not find their
> gondolas where they had moored them.
>   We often woke midwives and made them dress and go
> to deliver women who, when they arrived, called them
> fools. We did the same to the most celebrated physicians,
> whose slumbers we interrupted to send them to noble-
> men who, we told them, had suffered an apoplexy, and

we routed priests from their beds and packed them off to
pray for the souls of people in perfect health who, we said,
were at death's door.

In every street through which we passed we relentlessly
cut the bell cord hanging at every door; and when we
happened to find a door open because someone had
forgotten to shut it, we groped our way up the stairs and
terrified all the sleeping inmates by shouting at their
bedroom doors that the street door of the house was
open. And then we decamped, leaving the house door as
open as we had found it.

One very dark night we decided to overturn a big
marble table which was a sort of monument. The table
stood almost in the middle of the Campo Sant'Angelo. In
the days of the war which the Republic had fought against
the League of Cambrai, so the story ran, it was on this big
table that the commissaries had counted out their pay to
the recruits who enrolled in the service of St Mark.[32]

The sort of practical joking that Casanova records was a
common enough feature of eighteenth-century life, but in a
Venice given over to carnival and pleasure-seeking it seems to
have flourished with peculiar ferocity.

The building on the right as we enter the Campo Sant'-
Angelo is the sixteenth-century cloister of San Stefano, now
taken over by the Finance Offices. It is accustomed to such
invasions. In the mid-nineteenth century, when W. D.
Howells took to passing through the courtyard on his way to
the American consulate, it was occupied by the engineer corps
of the Austrian army. Today it can still be visited during office
hours, but we shall look in vain for the frescos that excited
Howells; the few surviving fragments have been removed to
the Correr Museum:

On one wall of this court are remains – very shadowy
remains indeed – of frescos painted by Pordenone at the
period of his fiercest rivalry with Titian; and it is said that
Pordenone, while he wrought upon the scenes of scrip-
tural story here represented, wore his sword and buckler,
in readiness to repel an attack which he feared from his

competitor. The story . . . gave a singular relish to our daily walk through the old cloister . . .[33]

PALAZZO BENZON

From the Campo Sant'Angelo another Calle del Spezier leads towards the Campo Manin. Before long it meets on the right the Rio Terrà degli Assassini, whose name carries its own warning. This was one of the areas of twisting streets and dark bridges where scores could be settled and unwary citizens helped to another life. In earlier centuries one might well have paused before crossing by night a bridge that had earned the name Ponte degli Assassini.

On the left-hand side, the Rio Terrà della Mandola takes us to the Fortuny Museum, once the home of Mariano Fortuny, the Spanish painter and designer whose exotic gowns, 'faithfully antique but markedly original', evoked for Proust all that was most gorgeous about the ancient city of the Doges. 'The Fortuny gown which Albertine was wearing that evening,' remarks Marcel in La Prisonnière, 'seemed to me the tempting phantom of that invisible Venice.'[34]

Behind the palace, an alleyway off the Calle Pesaro leads down to the Grand Canal beside the Palazzo Benzon. Like most of the palaces on the Grand Canal, this needs to be seen from the water. In its day it was a place of rendezvous for all that was most fashionable in Venetian society. Under the sway of the Countess Marina Querini-Benzon the salon which was held here welcomed among others Manzoni, Stendhal, and Byron. Byron, in particular. At a time when the Countess was already sixty, she is said to have excited enough interest in the poet for him to sustain a brief affair with her. Admittedly, Byron conferred the same distinction on a number of other women during his Venetian period – well over two hundred by his own reckoning – but it was a game gesture on the part of the Countess. She seems to have been an engaging figure – talented, witty, kind-hearted. Ten years later, when Longfellow visited her salon, she was still receiving company every evening from ten or eleven o'clock until three in the morning.

'The Venetian ladies are not handsome,' commented the poet, 'but they have a great deal of vivacity.'[35]

SAN LUCA

From the Calle Pesaro a tortuous couple of minutes' walk will bring us round to the front of the unlovely cinema which now stands on the site of the old Teatro di San Benedetto, once the most important theatre in Venice. The iron bridge in front of the cinema leads straight across to the church of San Luca. It was here in 1556 that Pietro Aretino was buried. His tomb was visited in the mid-seventeenth century by Sir John Reresby, a young Royalist who was keeping a comfortable distance between himself and the rigours of the Commonwealth by means of a well-timed Continental tour:

> In the church of St Luke lies interred Peter Aretin, that obscene profane poet, with this epitaph, till the inquisitors took it away, '*Qui jace Aretin, poeta Tusco, qui dice mal d'ogni uno fuora di Dio; scusandosi dicendo, Io no'l cognosco*' ('Here Aretin, the Tuscan poet, lies, who all the world abused but God, and why? he said he knew him not.')[36]

It is slightly surprising to find Aretino in a church at all. Not a man of devout life, he was said to have died from an apoplexy brought on by laughing at an obscene joke about his sister. After receiving extreme unction, he remarked with scant piety: 'Now that I'm well greased, you'd better keep the rats away.'

Of Italian writers associated with Venice Aretino is probably the most colourful. A native of Arezzo, he had been driven from Rome after some unguarded sonnets had found their way to a high Vatican official, who responded by trying to have the poet assassinated. At Mantua his savage pen again made life precarious, and in 1527 he turned to Venice. In its more liberal atmosphere his writings could offend with relative impunity. By flattering some and wounding others he managed to finance a life of prosperous debauchery, earning the friendship of Titian and Sansovino along the way. His final years were spent on the nearby Riva del Carbon.

Campo Manin

For those who wish to pay homage to a rather different hero of Venice, we are now only a few yards from the Campo Manin, a pleasant square spoiled by the ugly façade of the Cassa di Risparmio, on which even the statue of Manin seems to have turned its back. (Banks have a lot to answer for in Venice, as anyone who has stumbled into the Campo San Gallo will know.) It seems hard that the man who fought to restore the Republic should have been saddled with this monstrosity.

In the years before the Revolution of 1848 Daniele Manin lived with his wife and daughter in a house overlooking this square, which was then called San Paternian. Only moderately successful as a lawyer, Manin was brought to prominence by his part in the struggle against Austrian domination. It was he who on 22 March 1848 jumped on to a café table in the Piazza to proclaim the restored Republic. For the seventeen desperate months that followed he led the city's fight to remain independent. In the end, the Austrian blockade was too effective. By the summer of 1849 food was so scarce that one observer could note women among the crowd in the Campo San Giovanni e Paolo tearing off earrings and wedding rings in a frantic attempt to buy bread. To starvation was added cholera. As the summer wore on, the collapse of the Republic became inevitable. Starved, diseased, bombarded, it survived until the end of August. Finally, on 28 August, Manin sailed into exile aboard the French ship which was to carry him and his wife to Marseilles. By the time they made port, his wife was dead. Manin was left to eke out the last eight years of his life in Paris, making a modest living as a teacher of Italian.

Teatro Goldoni

The other side of the Cassa di Risparmio presents an altogether more acceptable face to the lively Campo San Luca. As we walk round into the square, we notice at once the change in tempo that marks the start of Venice's main commercial district. From the middle of the square a left turn beside another bank, followed by a right turn into the Calle del Teatro – opposite yet another bank – will take us to the steps of the Teatro Goldoni. In spite of the unattractive façade with which various changes and restorations have left it, the theatre has a venerable past. Built by the Vendramin family in the seventeenth century, it enjoyed the great age of Venetian theatre and is now one of the oldest surviving playhouses in the city. On 10 October 1786 it was visited by Goethe. The entry in his Journal shows how well he understood the basis of Goldoni's popularity:

> At last I have seen a real comedy! At the Teatro San Luca today they played *Le Baruffe Chiozzotte*, one of the few plays by Goldoni which is still performed. The title might be roughly translated as *The Scuffles and Brawls in Chioggia*. The characters are all natives of that town, fishermen and their wives, sisters and daughters. The habitual to-do made by these people, their quarrels, their outbursts of temper, their good nature, superficiality, wit, humour and natural behaviour – all these were excellently imitated. I was in Chioggia only yesterday, so their faces were still vivid in my mind's eye and their voices still ringing in my ears. . . .
>
> I have never in my life witnessed such an ecstasy of joy as that shown by the audience when they saw themselves and their families so realistically portrayed on the stage. They shouted with laughter and approval from beginning to end.[37]

CAMPO SAN SALVADOR

From the Calle del Teatro it is only a step to the bustling Campo San Salvador, a favourite meeting-place in the evenings for Venetian teenagers. The church, which contains the tomb of Caterina Cornaro, Queen of Cyprus, is now as staid a place of worship as any in Venice – more so than most perhaps, since even Titian's superb *Annunciation* attracts only a modest flow of tourists – but like many such places it had a rather different reputation in the eighteenth century. Maurice Andrieux quotes one of the Inquisition spies, whose report is dated 28 June 1771: 'the church of San Salvatore is being defiled by the mixed crowds of women who go there, not to hear Mass, but to be seen and accosted. God-fearing persons frequently remark that this church has turned into a brothel.'[38]

A more conscientious tourist than most, L. P. Hartley's Eustace decides to make San Salvatore the subject of an experiment:

> Hitherto Eustace had been a systematic sight-seer, choosing his quarry beforehand and going straight to it. But privately he felt that this method was touristy and crude: as the book said, one should be a wanderer in Venice, one should drift, one should take the object of one's search by surprise, not antagonise it by a vulgar frontal attack. Left alone, not hunted and cornered, the church would just 'occur'; against shock-tactics it would surely erect all its defences and withhold its message. Eustace determined that his discovery of the church of San Salvatore, which housed two important Titians, should be utterly unpremeditated. He would just look round and find himself there, and the picture, surprised out of a day-dream, would tell him something it would never have told in answer to a direct question.[39]

Unfortunately, Eustace's knowledge of the streets of Venice is not up to taking churches by surprise and San Salvatore continues to guard its secret.

Campo San Bartolomeo

Past the side-entrance of the church the crowded Merceria San Salvador leads up towards the Piazza. It is one of the group of streets which used to be the preserve of the haberdashers' shops, or *mercerie*. Their starting-point is a short way beyond

San Salvador at the Campo San Bartolomeo, which for the past hundred years has been dominated by the bronze statue of Carlo Goldoni. Erected in 1883, it was the occasion of an unmemorable poem by Browning – one of the few that bears directly on the city in which he passed his final days. It was to this vivid, noisy square that W. D. Howells moved in March 1862, towards the end of his first winter in Venice. Surrounded by the cages of screaming finches, canaries, blackbirds, and parrots which hung from the neighbouring balconies, he was well placed to observe the more raucous side of Venetian life. Looking down from his window, he could also turn his attention to the assorted figures gathered in the square below,

> to the placid dandies about the door of the caffè; to the tide of passers from the Merceria; the smooth-shaven Venetians of other days, and the bearded Venetians of these; the dark-eyed, white-faced Venetian girls, hooped in cruel disproportion to the narrow streets, but richly clad, and moving with southern grace; the files of heavily burdened soldiers; the little policemen loitering lazily about with their swords at their sides, and in their spotless Austrian uniforms.[40]

The scene described by Howells barely hints at the undercurrent of tension that pervaded Venetian social life during the years of his residence there. In 1797 Venice had been handed over to Austria by Napoleon. Apart from the events of 1848–9 and a ten year interval from 1805 to 1815, she had remained under Austrian domination ever since. The result was an abiding hostility that expressed itself in continual acts of petty tyranny by the Austrians and an unrelenting show of resentment by the Italians. This incident, recalled by George Sand, is perhaps not entirely typical either in the nature of the offence or in its comparatively happy ending, but it conveys the bitter tone of relations between the two communities:

> One evening when I was in the gondola moored at a jetty, waiting while my old boatman brought back something or other that I had told him to go and fetch, I heard the

sound of the *felze*, that is to say the cabin of the gondola, being sprinkled by a passer-by whom I supposed to be either drunk or distracted.

Since the shutters were closed, I had nothing to fear from this unseemly aspersion. Then I heard the hoarse voice of Catulle calling out:

'*Porco di Tedesco!* so you think you can pollute my gondola! Do you take it for a lamppost?'

'Know,' replied the other in bad Italian, 'that I am an officer in the service of His Austrian Majesty, and that I have a perfect right to piss on your gondola if I so choose.'

'But there is a lady in my gondola!' cried the gondolier.

Then the Austrian officer, who was not drunk at all, came to open the door of the *felze*, and, looking at me, said:

'The signora has had the *gentilezza e la prudenza* to keep quiet: she has done well. As for you, tomorrow you will go to prison, and you are very lucky that I don't run my sword through your body.'

And poor Catulle really would have been in prison if I had not interceded for him, saying that he was tipsy and seeming to take as an honour what the Austrian had deigned to let fall on my gondola.[41]

As it happens, the Campo San Bartolomeo was itself the scene of one of the last despairing acts of revolt against the surrender of the Republic to Napoleon. On the night of 12/13 May 1797 outraged Venetians rampaged through the streets intent on sacking the houses of those who were felt to have betrayed the Republic. The riot gained strength, and a local commander moved up artillery to the top of the Rialto bridge. As the crowd surged past the church of San Bartolomeo, a blast from the guns reduced the last Republicans to a bloody scattering of limbs along the Salizzada. As Giuseppe Tassini puts it, in a pardonable flight of rhetoric: 'Fatal destiny that the cannon of St Mark should loose their thunder for the last time not against the enemies of Venice but against her sons.'[42]

MERCERIE

The streets which lead from the Campo San Bartolomeo back to San Marco are among the busiest in Venice, and have been for centuries. In 1645 John Evelyn was entranced by the luxury and colour of their display. He had reached Venice in high summer, just half way through the long continental tour that was to keep him out of England for most of the decade. He could not have timed it more adroitly. From the savageries of a country laid waste by Civil War he had escaped to something infinitely more congenial:

> Hence I pass'd through the *Merceria*, which I take to be the most delicious streete in the World for the sweetnesse of it, being all the way on both sides, continualy tapissry'd as it were, with Cloth of Gold, rich Damasks & other silks, which the shops expose & hang before their houses from the first floore, & with that variety, that for neere half the yeare, which I spent chiefly in this citty, I hardly remember to have seene the same piece twice exposd, to this add the perfumers & Apothecaries shops, and the innumerable cages of Nightingals, which they keepe, that entertaines you with their melody from shop to shop, so as shutting your Eyes, you would imagine your selfe in the Country, when indeede you are in the middle of the Sea.[43]

Thirty years after Evelyn's visit the Mercerie acquired even greater prestige when they became the first streets in the city to be paved in stone. Looking back to the Venice of his youth, Goldoni writes nostalgically in his memoirs of the flags outside the haberdashers' shops, chiselled to prevent customers slipping in the wet.

At a busy intersection just short of St Mark's stands the sixteenth-century church of San Giuliano, notable as the only church in Venice which can be walked all the way round. It was rebuilt at the expense of a scholar and physician called Tommaso Rangone, partly to the glory of God, partly to the glory of himself. He seems to have had little sympathy with the Venetian ethic of anonymity; above the main door, in much the place where one might expect an image of the

Redeemer, sits a handsome statue of him by Sansovino, surrounded by symbols of his scientific and literary achievements. The church was later the scene of his funeral, an elaborate affair in which a train of precious items was borne in the wake of his coffin, including all the books he had written, open at pages specified by him in advance. To ensure the right tone, he also stipulated what clothes his librarian should wear for the occasion. He had a long life, but not, perhaps, as long as he expected; his main professional claim was to teach people to live to the age of 120.

Just before reaching the arch of the clock tower, we pass on the right the Sottoportico del Cappello, now the entrance to a glass factory. Above it is a relief of the old woman who was credited with frustrating the revolt of Baiamonte Tiepolo in 1310. Coryate politely calls her a maid and explains that she happened to be using a pestle and mortar at the time when the rebel forces reached the edge of the Piazza. As she looked out of the window to see what was happening,

> her pestell which she then held in her hand, not intending any hurt with it, fell casually much against her will upon the head of the Ring-leader of this company, which strooke out his braines, and so by that dismall chance hee died in the place, being defeated of the effect of his project, for the execution whereof he assembled so many armed men . . .[44]

At the time of Coryate's visit tourists were still being shown the window from which the pestle fell; but the story had already drifted clear of reality. It was not Baiamonte whom the old woman killed but his standard-bearer, and she herself, according to other versions, was less undesigning than Coryate suggests. Certainly, she was treated as a heroine by the Republic. In recompense she asked that her rent should never be raised and that on feast days she should be granted permission to hang from her window the standard of St Mark. In his history of Venice John Julius Norwich notes that a century and a half later one of the old woman's descendants was still able to make a successful appeal against any increase in the rent.

CAMPO SAN GALLO

Before retiring to a café, there is one more place to visit – a penance, this time, rather than a pleasure. The easiest way to reach it, tucked away behind the Procuratie Vecchie, is to enter the Piazza, walk along the arcade, then leave again by the sottoportico beside the Olivetti showroom. The street this takes us down is named after the *cavalletto* where horses were stabled in the fourteenth century for hire by visitors to the city. At the end of it is what remains of the Campo San Gallo. This charmless little spot is one of Venice's disaster stories. The shabby cinema, now being renovated, is of minor importance. What destroyed the square was the absurd pair of banks, heavy, humourless and quite alien to the spirit of Venetian architecture. The house where Canova died was an incidental casualty of this sad fiasco.

For an image of the life and colour that have been lost we can turn to Théophile Gautier. It was here that on a summer evening in 1850 he and his Italian mistress came to dine at a small German restaurant:

We had our meal in the open air, under an awning of white and saffron stripes, side by side with French painters, German artists and Austrian officers. . . .

In the middle of the campo was a well-head where the women of the neighbourhood and the water-carriers came at certain hours to draw water. At the far end stood a small church emblazoned with the arms of the Patriarch of Venice, and from its doorway, closed off by a red curtain, came a vague odour of incense and the sound of prayers and organ music – the one mingling with the kitchen smells of the restaurant, the other with the discussions of art and philosophy. . . .

Bare-headed girls with strikingly coloured shawls went by, a fan in their hand and a smile on their lips, pushing back the flounces of their dresses with a delicate foot. Instead of going into the church, they took the little alley which leads from the Campo San Gallo to the Piazza. They will go into the church later, when there is no one else for them to love but God – that final object of a woman's passion.[45]

Before we return to the Piazza, a last, short detour will take us to the Ponte dei Fuseri, where a plaque indicates the palace in which Goethe stayed from 28 September to 14 October 1786. He had come to Venice at the start of the great Italian journey which was to change both his life and his thought. His arrival is marked in the journal by a sigh of relief: 'So now, thank God, Venice is no longer a mere word to me, an empty name . . .'[46] It is, in its way, a striking tribute. How many other famous cities can match the fantasies their names evoke?

PIAZZA SAN MARCO

PALAZZO PATRIARCALE

RIO DI PALAZZO

BRIDGE OF SIGHS

PRISONS

PONTE DELLA PAGLIA

PIAZZETTA DEI LEONCINI (GIOVANNI XXIII)

BASILICA DI SAN MARCO

PALAZZO DUCALE (DOGE'S PALACE)

MOLO

PORTA DELLA CARTA

LOGGETTA

PIAZZETTA DI SAN MARCO

Merceria d. Orologio

TORRE DELL' OROLOGIO

CAMPANILE DI SAN MARCO

PROCURATIE VECCHIE

PIAZZA SAN MARCO

PROCURATIE NUOVE

ALA NAPOLEONICA

MUSEO CORRER

GIARDINETTI REALI

yards 0

0 metres

25

50

75

100

25

50

75

100

4

PIAZZA SAN MARCO

PIAZZA

The more celebrated the place, the less interesting is likely to
be the traveller's description of it. Tedious accounts of the
wonders of St Mark's Square would comfortably fill a volume
of their own. Even the most evocative writing dwindles to
banality beside the fabulous images with which the reader's
mind is already stocked. And in turn the fabulous images pale
before the reality. 'Indeed,' writes Max Beerbohm, 'I should
not envy the soul of one who at first sight of such strange
loveliness found anything to say.' But in a sceptical world, he
adds, some evidence of love is demanded:

> Well, then, for me the church has hardly the effect of a
> building; of a garden, rather; an Eastern garden that had
> been by some Christian miracle petrified just when the
> flowers were fading, so that its beauty should last forever
> to the glory of Christ, and of S. Mark. But Mohammed
> had walked there, and his spirit haunts it yet, ranging
> from dome to dome, from cornice to cornice, unafraid of
> the Saint's own lion which, haloed, mounts golden guard
> in the midst, against a starred blue background; and one

almost wonders that among those stars no crescent is gleaming.[1]

For upwards of three centuries it has been impossible to write of the Piazza without a consciousness of all that has been written of it before. It is one of the attractions of Coryate's *Crudities* that he writes with a vivid conviction of telling things for the first time. The Piazza is 'the fairest place of all the citie':

> Truely such is the stupendious (to use a strange Epitheton for so strange and rare a place as this) glory of it, that at my first entrance thereof it did even amaze or rather ravish my senses. For here is the greatest magnificence of architecture to be seene, that any place under the sunne doth yeelde. Here you may both see all manner of fashions of attire, and heare all the languages of Christen-dome, besides those that are spoken by the barbarous Ethnickes; the frequencie of people being so great twise a day, betwixt six of the clocke in the afternoon and eight, that (as an elegant writer saith of it) a man may very properly call it rather Orbis than Urbis forum, that is a market place of the world, not of the citie.[2]

The exciting confusion of races was something later travellers continued to remark upon. When Effie Ruskin, newly married, reached Venice in 1849, it was still a noticeable feature of the Piazza. Her wide-eyed delight in the scene provides an appealing link with Coryate across the centuries of more self-conscious observers. She wrote to her mother on 13 November, a few days after she and Ruskin had arrived:

> The place is like a vast drawing room lighted enough by the gas from the arcades all round the square under which sit all the Ladies & gentlemen at their coffee, iced water and cigars with a dense crowd in the centre of men, women, children, soldiers, Turks, magnificent Greek costumes and sky above studded with innumerable twinkling stars. I was walking there with John last night till past eight without any bonnet but my hair dressed – walking about like all the rest amongst the crowd, taking

our coffee under the Arcade and enjoying ourselves
extremely.[3]

Her enthusiasm was perhaps a little unguarded. Before the end
of the month an anxious letter had arrived from Ruskin's
father warning against the possible impropriety of walking in
public without a bonnet.

Effie's first impressions had been anticipated by Napoleon,
who called the Piazza 'the finest drawing room in Europe'.
The same image reappears as a passing reference in Henry
James's novel *The Princess Casamassima*, but for a more detailed
picture we can turn to one of his slightly later books. The
complacent narrator of *The Aspern Papers* makes a habit of
repairing to the Piazza in the early evening:

> I sat in front of Florian's *café*, eating ices, listening to
> music, talking with acquaintances: the traveller will re-
> member how the immense cluster of tables and little
> chairs stretches like a promontory into the smooth lake of
> the Piazza. The whole place, of a summer's evening,
> under the stars and with all the lamps, all the voices and
> light footsteps on the marble (the only sounds of the
> arcades that enclose it), is like an open-air saloon dedi-
> cated to cooling drinks and to a still finer degustation –
> that of the exquisite impressions received during the day.
> When I did not prefer to keep mine to myself there was
> always a stray tourist, disencumbered of his Bädeker, to
> discuss them with, or some domesticated painter rejoic-
> ing in the return of the season of strong effects. The
> wonderful church, with its low domes and bristling
> embroideries, the mystery of its mosaic and sculpture,
> looked ghostly in the tempered gloom, and the sea-breeze
> passed between the twin columns of the Piazzetta, the
> lintels of a door no longer guarded, as gently as if a rich
> curtain were swaying there.[4]

FLORIAN'S

In books it is always Florian's that people choose – reasonably
enough. E. V. Lucas quotes an advertisement for the café in

the Piazza musical programme just before the First World War: 'the oldest and most aristocratic establishment of its kind in Venice, it can count among its clients, since 1720, Byron, Goethe, Rousseau, Canova, Dumas, and Moor', the last of these apparently referring to the Moore who was Byron's friend and biographer.

Coffee had first been brought to the attention of the Venetians in 1585 when Gianfrancesco Morosini, who was *bailo* in Constantinople, reported to the Senate that the Turks were accustomed to drink 'a black water, boiled up as hot as they can bear it, which is distilled from a seed they call *kahvé* and which they say has the property of making a man stay awake'. By the middle of the next century coffee was on sale in Venice as a medicine. Its popularity increased, imports rose, and in 1683 the first coffee shop opened under the Procuratie Nuove, where Florian's still sets out its tables. 'The arcade outside Florian's,' remarks Murray in 1877, 'is the rendezvous of the Venetian *beau monde* in the warm summer evenings, when the military band plays'. Even during the period of Austrian occupation the café retained its dignity. While Quadri's, patronized by the Austrians, was shunned by good Venetians, Florian's managed to establish itself as neutral ground where it was acceptable for either nationality to be seen.

In 1850, sixteen years before the end of the Austrian occupation, Théophile Gautier describes how the upper-class Venetian women are occasionally tempted as far as Florian's on days of unusual mildness. In general, he says, they are reluctant to risk themselves out of doors:

If there is one thing in the world that is unashamedly indolent and lazy, it is the Venetian women of the upper classes. The use of the gondola has made them unaccustomed to walking. They scarcely know how to put one foot in front of the other. For them to risk themselves out of doors requires a rare conjunction of atmospheric circumstances, even in this mild and gentle climate. The sirocco, the sun, a cloud that threatens rain, too cool a breeze from the sea – any of these is reason enough for them to stay at home. The most trifling thing prostrates them, the most trifling thing fatigues them, and their greatest exercise is to go to the couch on their balcony and inhale the scent of one of the large flowers which bloom so well in the warm, humid air of Venice. This untroubled and secluded life gives them an immaculate and unvarnished pallor, an incredible delicacy of complexion.

When, by chance, there is the sort of exceptional weather we call in France *temps de demoiselle*, some of them take two or three turns round the Piazza at the time when the military band is playing its evening symphony, then settle down for a long rest outside Florian's with a glass of water turned opal in colour by a drop of aniseed, accompanied by their husbands, brothers or *cavalieri serventi*.[5]

For us, too, Florian's is a convenient place from which to survey the Piazza. Rhapsodies about churches, even about a church as fantastic as St Mark's, tend to be peculiarly indigestible. More appealing than Ruskin's description of the magnificence of the basilica's exterior is his mordant paragraph on the indifference to it of the local populace:

And what effect has this splendour on those who pass beneath it? You may walk from sunrise to sunset, to and fro, before the gateway of St Mark's, and you will not see an eye lifted to it, not a countenance brightened by it. Priest and layman, soldier and civilian, rich and poor, pass by it alike regardlessly. Up to the very recesses of the porches, the meanest tradesmen of the city push their counters; nay, the foundations of its pillars are themselves the seats – not 'of them that sell doves' for sacrifice, but of the vendors of toys and caricatures. Round the whole square in front of the church there is almost a continuous line of cafés, where the idle Venetians of the middle classes lounge, and read empty journals; in its centre the Austrian bands play during the time of vespers, their martial music jarring with the organ notes, – the march drowning the miserere, and the sullen crowd thickening round them, – a crowd, which, if it had its will, would

stiletto every soldier that pipes to it. And in the recesses of
the porches, all day long, knots of men of the lowest
classes, unemployed and listless, lie basking in the sun like
lizards; and unregarded children – every heavy glance of
their young eyes full of desperation and stony depravity,
and their throats hoarse with cursing, – gamble, and
fight, and snarl, and sleep, hour after hour, clashing their
bruised centesimi upon the marble ledges of the church
porch. And the images of Christ and His angels look
down upon it continually.[6]

Popular indifference could pose a threat that was physical as
well as moral. E. V. Lucas describes how in 1889 his guide
casually chipped off a few pieces of mosaic with his knife to sell
to tourists.

They do things differently today. Nonetheless, Ruskin's
diatribe would only need up-dating. Many years later he
himself added a tart footnote about the way his writings had
been received. It provides a sardonic cameo of Victorian
travellers in Venice, who have paid no attention to what he
said but have admired his manner of saying it:

and, as far as they found the things I spoke of amusing to
themselves, they have deigned for a couple of days or so
to look at them, – helped always through the tedium of
the business by due quantity of ices at Florian's, music by
moonlight on the Grand Canal, paper lamps and the
English papers and magazines at M. Ongania's, with such
illumination as those New Lamps contain – Lunar or
Gaseous, enabling pursy Britannia to compare, at her
ease, her own culminating and co-operate Prosperity and
Virtue with the past wickedness and present out-of-
pocketness of the umquhile Queen of the Sea.[7]

And yet if we try to think of the basilica on a summer
afternoon without its milling tourists and local hucksters, does
it gain or lose? To have the Parthenon to ourselves or Chartres
cathedral or the Taj Mahal would be an imaginative luxury;
but St Mark's is different. The French novelist Michel Butor
has pointed out that while many ancient monuments seem

profaned by the rout of tourists who fall upon them, these same tourists are as necessary to the façade of St Mark's as water is to the façades of the city's palaces:

> The basilica, like the city around it, has nothing to fear from this fauna or from our own frivolity; it was born under the perpetual gaze of the visitor, and so it has continued. Its artists have worked amid the chatter of sailors and merchants. Since the beginning of the 13th century, this façade has been a shop window, a show case for antiques. The shops under the arcades are in reality a continuation of it.[8]

St Mark's

By a happy chance the one original mosaic that has survived in the five arches over the doorways of St Mark's is a thirteenth-century portrayal of the translation of the body of the saint himself to the basilica. In the early days of Venice the city's patron saint was St Theodore. His displacement by St Mark was the result of an enterprising piece of theft in the ninth century. Augustus Hare tells the traditional story:

> The translation of the body of S. Mark to Venice is said to have been caused by the rapacity of the King of Alexandria, who plundered the church where he was enshrined in that city to adorn his own palace. Two Venetian sea-captains who were then at Alexandria implored to be allowed to remove the relics of the saint to a place of safety, and at last the priests, fearful of further desecration, consented. 'They placed the corpse in a large basket covered with herbs and swine's flesh which the Mussulmans hold in horror, and the bearers were directed to cry *Khwazir* (pork), to all who should ask questions or approach to search. In this manner they reached the vessel. The body was enveloped in the sails, and suspended to the mainmast till the moment of departure, for it was necessary to conceal this precious booty from those who might come to clear the vessel in the roads. At last

the Venetians quitted the shore full of joy. They were hardly in the open sea when a great storm arose. We are assured that S. Mark then appeared to the captain and warned him to strike all his sails immediately, lest the ship, driven before the wind, should be wrecked upon hidden rocks. They owed their safety to this miracle.'⁹

It seems unlikely that the two sea-captains were as disinterested as this makes them sound. Legend had long ago given Venice a stake in St Mark, since the Evangelist had stopped at the site of the unborn city on his way back from Aquileia to Rome and been visited at the time by an angel who greeted him with the words, *Pax tibi, Marce evangelista meus. Hic requiescet corpus tuum.*' This was not the sort of prediction that the predatory Venetians were inclined to leave unfulfilled. St Theodore, for all his virtues – and he can still be seen with his crocodile on one of the columns of the Piazzetta – was scarcely a first-class saint, and Venice deserved nothing less.

In the vestibule of the church Thomas Mowbray, Duke of Norfolk, was buried after he had died in Venice in 1399. This is the same Mowbray whose quarrel with Bolingbroke and subsequent banishment by Richard II were dramatized in Shakespeare's play:

> The sly slow hours shall not determinate
> The dateless limit of thy dear exile;
> The hopeless words of 'never to return'
> Breathe I against thee, upon pain of life.

Bolingbroke later returned to depose Richard and become Henry IV. Mowbray lived less than a year in exile before he died of the plague here in Venice at the end of a pilgrimage to the Holy Land. In the sixteenth century his descendants retrieved his ashes and brought them back to rest in England.

The shadowy interior of the church, over-arched by gold mosaics, is a haunting place, especially in winter, when the crowd of tourists thins and the smoking candles light obscure corners with a flickering glow. But the connoisseur of such things might try to catch St Mark's on an afternoon in late summer at the moment suggested by Théophile Gautier:

At certain hours, when the shadows thicken and the sun only casts one ray of light obliquely under the vaults of the cupolas, strange effects rise for the eye of the poet and visionary. Brazen lightnings flash suddenly from the golden backgrounds. Little cubes of crystal gleam here and there like the sunlit sea: the outlines of the figures tremble in their golden field; the silhouettes which were just before so clearly marked become troubled and mingled to the eye. The harsh folds on the dalmatics seem to soften and take movement; mysterious life glides into these motionless Byzantine figures; fixed eyes turn, arms with Egyptian hieratic gestures move, sealed feet begin to walk; the eight wings of cherubim revolve like wheels; the angels unfold the long wings of azure and purple which an implacable mosaic holds to the wall . . .[10]

A strange sight to see the youthful saints smiling with their porphyry lips. The effect, says Gautier, is of a cathedral that 'seems as if it belonged to a pre-Christian Christianity, to a Church founded before religion existed'.

Before we begin, in Beckford's words, to pry about the great church of St Mark, it is worth pausing at the door to look back at the mosaic of the Apocalypse above the main entrance. It seems that while working on this mosaic in 1563 the Zuccato brothers had in places simplified their task by using paint. The enmity of a fellow mosaic worker revealed this to the Procurators and an inspection was held in which Titian, Tintoretto, and Veronese all took part. In spite of the committee's praise for the quality of the mosaic, the charge was proved. Francesco Zuccato was temporarily deprived of his salary and ordered to rework the painted areas at his own expense. It was on this episode that George Sand based her novel *Les maîtres mosaïstes*.

On the right-hand side of the church, as one looks towards the altar, is the baptistery, containing the tomb of Andrea Dandolo (1354), which E. V. Lucas thought 'one of the most beautiful things in Venice'. It is, writes Ruskin, 'like a narrow couch set beside the window, low-roofed and curtained, so that it might seem, but that it is some height above the pavement, to have been drawn towards the window, that the sleeper might be wakened early.'[11] Dandolo was the last of the Doges to be buried in St Mark's, and it is to him that we owe an early history of Venice in Latin, the *Chronicon Venetum*.

Readers of Proust will already have turned their attention to the baptistery floor. It was the precise sensation of standing on two of its uneven stones that held the key to all the images of Venice which his narrator, Marcel, had tried vainly to recapture. Years later, in a moment of deep depression, Marcel stumbles one afternoon in the entrance-way to the Hôtel de Guermantes. The sensation of the uneven paving-stones, suddenly repeated, unlocks this fragment of his past, and the whole of Venice comes back to him. It brings a rush of happiness more vivid than any effort of memory, restoring his faith in the literary task that was to become *À la recherche du temps perdu*.

Just beyond the baptistery is the basilica's Treasury, which at the end of the sixteenth century contained three unicorn horns, now lost. Visiting the Treasury some fifty years later, John Evelyn mentions only two, but his attitude to the relics was casual. He seems little moved by the 'divers heads of Saints, inchas'd in Gold' that were shown him by favour of the French ambassador, and his list of subordinate relics is unceremonious:

> Also a small Ampulla or glasse of B: Saviou[r]s blood, as they fancy: A greate morcell of the real Crosse, one of the nailes, a Thorne, a fragment of the Column to which our Lord was bound, when Scourged: The Labbarum or Ensigne of victorious *Constantine*, a piece of St *Lukes* arme, a rib of St *Stephen*, a finger of Mary Magdalene & a world of Reliques I could not remember.[12]

In a sceptical age, when lesser churches are sometimes diffident about their relics, St Mark's until recently displayed a satisfying range of venerable objects. This is no longer the case, and when the Sanctuary reopens after its renovation, it will probably be purged of even more of its riches.

The sacristy is difficult to get into, but we can at least, by paying to have a look at the Pala d'Oro, see Sansovino's door to it in the left-hand niche of the apse. Around the frame are bronze reliefs of Sansovino himself, Titian, and Aretino. Aretino is at the top right with prominent nose and flowing beard, Titian opposite and Sansovino below him.

The most exciting view of the interior of the church, and certainly of its mosaics, is to be had from the gallery, which also gives access to the Loggia. The prospect is splendid, but the bronze horses, replaced by replicas, have now been withdrawn to a display room inside. Those who touched the originals – 'so set,' Moryson tells us, 'as if at the first step they would leape into the market place' – will be conscious of a pang of disappointment.

Looking out across the Piazza, we share the view with a fair number of pigeons as well as with other tourists. In recent years few people have had much to say for these well-fed birds. Oscar Wilde's Dorian Gray was an exception. Stretched on his sofa, he reads some lines of Gautier and thinks back to his stay in Venice: 'The sudden flashes of colour reminded him of the gleam of the opal-and-iris-throated birds that flutter round the tall honeycombed Campanile, or stalk, with such stately grace, through the dim, dust-stained arcades.'[13]

According to tradition, it was from the gallery where we are standing that the original pigeons were released on Palm Sunday, weighted by pieces of paper tied to their legs. Most of them ended up on the dinner table as part of the Doge's Easter largesse to the populace, but the rugged survivors were felt to have earned St Mark's protection. So year by year a few more pigeons found refuge among the domes of the basilica. They have since grown numerous, and the enthusiasm of most tourists for the birds is short-lived, but as the average visitor now spends less than twenty-four hours in the city they still have plenty of friends. James Morris quotes an early Baedeker which makes little effort to conceal its distaste for the pigeon-fanciers: 'those whose ambitions lean in that direction,' it remarks, 'may have themselves photographed covered with the birds.' Even before the age of photographs, the pigeons were a popular diversion. In 1851 Elizabeth Barrett Browning, in Venice with Robert, describes their son in a letter to her sister: 'He has made friends with the "holy pigeons", & they were surrounding him like a cloud today for the sake of his piece of bread . . . he stamping & crying out for rapture in the grand piazza.'[14]

THE CLOCK TOWER

The northern end of the Loggia offers an excellent view of the clock tower, which was built at the end of the fifteenth century. By the time Thomas Coryate came to Venice in 1608, the dangers of its spectacular system of striking the hours should have been better appreciated than they were. After a brief description of the clock, Coryate goes on:

> At which clocke there fell out a very tragicall and rufull accident on the twenty fifth day of July being munday about nine of the clocke in the morning, which was this. A certaine fellow that had the charge to looke to the clocke, was very busie about the bell, according to his usual custome every day, to the end to amend something in it that was amisse. But in the meane time one of those wilde men that at the quarters of the howers doe use to strike the bell, strooke the man in the head with his brazen hammer, giving him such a violent blow, that therewith he fel down dead presently in the place, and never spake more. Surely I will not justifie this for an undoubted truth, because I saw it not. For I was at that time in the Dukes Palace observing of matters: but as soone as I came forth some of my country-men that tolde me they saw the matter with there owne eies, reported it unto me, and advised me to mention it in my journall for a most lamentable chance.[15]

True or not, the incident found its way into popular legend. Forty years later Evelyn reports talking to 'an honest merchant' who also claimed to have witnessed the event.

Along the south side of the piazza run the Procuratie Nuove. Once the residence of the procurators of St Mark, later a palace for Napoleon, they now house the rooms of the Correr Museum. (Those who have shivered round this intriguing museum in winter-time should note that its attractions now include a modern central heating system.) To give an idea of the museum's range, it is enough to say that it exhibits items as diverse as Jacopo de Barbari's map of Venice, Canova's *Daedalus and Icarus*, Giuliana di Collalto's sarcophagus (see p. 210), a brocaded ducal cap dating from the fifteenth century, a wide range of coins, including a zecchino with the portrait of Marin Falier, sundry lions of St Mark, and a signboard of the Barbers' Guild. All this without entering the fine picture gallery, where among the madonnas and saints Carpaccio's two Venetian women sit staring with terrible weariness from their balcony. It is a museum that well repays a visit.

CAMPANILE

Rising beside the windows at the far end of the museum is the massive structure of the campanile. For as long as tourists have visited Venice, they have been recommending what Coryate called 'the fairest and goodliest prospect that is (I thinke) in all the world'. It was here that Galileo demonstrated his telescope to the Doge and Goethe first saw the sea. Convinced, like William Beckford, that the campanile would outlast every other monument in the Piazza, the tourists continued to climb its ramps and wonder at the view – until one summer's morning in 1902. A brief dispatch from Reuters, dated VENICE, 14 July (10.40 AM) carried the news:

> The Campanile of St. Mark's Cathedral, 98 metres high (about 318 feet), has just fallen down on to the Piazza.
>
> It collapsed where it stood, and is now a heap of ruins.
>
> The cathedral and the Doge's Palace are quite safe. Only a corner of the royal palace is damaged.
>
> It is believed, but it is not certain, that there has been no loss of life.
>
> A cordon of troops is keeping the Piazza clear.

The circumstances of the collapse were described in *The Times* a few days later when a reader sent in the account received by him from an American architect who had been there at the time:

> Workmen had been repointing the Campanile, and had discovered a bad crack starting from the crown of the second arched window on the corner towards St Mark's, and extending through the sixth window. This crack had shown signs of opening further, and they feared small fragments falling on the crowded Piazza; so the music was quietly stopped in the hope that the crowd would naturally disperse. The effect was exactly the opposite of that desired. Every one rushed to the Piazza. At eleven I was under the tower which rose in the dim moonlight. The crack was distinctly visible even in this half light, but apparently menaced only a corner of the tower. On Monday, early, the Campanile was resplendent in the sunshine. At nine my little girl Katharine went off with her horns of corn to feed the pigeons. Mrs – was at St Laccana, and I was near the Rialto sketching. The golden Angel on the tower was shining far away. Suddenly I saw it slowly sink directly downward behind a line of roofs, and a dense grey dust rose in clouds. At once a crowd of people began running across the Rialto towards the Piazza, and I ordered my gondolier to the Piazzetta. On arrival the sight was pitiful. Of that splendid shaft all that remained was a mound of white dust, spreading to the walls of St Mark's.[16]

The campanile is not the sort of thing that can be knocked down to suit an architectural fancy, but when it had fallen of its own accord it is questionable whether the Venetians need have been quite so keen to rebuild it. Osbert Sitwell was one of many who had reservations. Writing of a winter visit to Venice, he remarks:

> The blue sky seemed very pale and far off. Above, the sun flashed its wings on the golden triangular edgings of the Campanile, but only succeeded in emphasizing the discrepancy between the magnificence of the top of it and the square, brick-built tower itself. It was impossible, I

found, not to regret this one piece of common sense in an otherwise magical world: especially since I could remember the square in a much rarer condition, when, as I now know, it was more beautiful than it is at present or had been during a thousand years. For at the time of my first visit to Venice, the Campanile was then in process of being rebuilt, and stood no higher than St Mark's Library.[17]

The bells of the reconstructed campanile play little part in the daily life of the city, but this was not always the case. There were five in all, each with a distinct function described by Horatio Brown:

> The *Marangona* was the great bell of the city marking the main moments of the day; it rang at sunrise, at *Ave Maria* for the cessation of work, and at midnight. The *Trottiera* summoned the senate to its sittings; the *Ringhiera* tolled for those about to die by the hand of justice. The *Mezza Terza* and the *Nona* announced other important hours; the *Nona*, for example, rang midday. All these bells were rung either by hammer in the bell-chamber or by rope from the base of the Campanile. The holes through which the bell-ropes passed were coated with thick bottle-glass to diminish the wear and tear. In the fall of the tower the *Marangona* [which still survives] was but little injured; the rest were broken.[18]

Apart from the campanile itself, the only other building of importance to suffer in the disaster was Sansovino's Loggetta at the base of the campanile, and this too was reconstructed. Sansovino was not always lucky with his buildings in Venice. While the Library of St Mark was under construction in 1545, the vault of the great Hall suddenly collapsed, weakened by the hard December frost. The Republic did not expect errors from its City Architect. Sansovino was consigned to prison, where he remained until the intercession of Aretino and Titian secured his release. In the event, he seems to have weathered the experience pretty well, living on in Venice for another twenty-five years. Vasari tells us that his digestion was so remarkable that he could cope with more or less anything, 'often eating as many as three cucumbers at a time with half a lemon in his extreme old age'.

The National Library that finally came into being is a monument to his genius. Among other treasures in its possession are the books which Petrarch gave to Venice. At the time no one seems to have been much impressed by this handsome prize and the books were left to moulder for a century and a half.

PIAZZETTA

The Piazzetta acquired its most distinctive characteristic towards the end of the twelfth century when the two monolithic columns were brought here from the east and set in place, one surmounted by St Theodore and his crocodile, the other by the winged lion of St Mark. The engineer who erected them claimed as his reward the right to set up gambling booths between them, but, according to the story, the Council immediately tried to neutralize the privilege by appointing this as the place of public execution, thereby making it ill-omened. If this was the intention, it failed; Coryate reports that dicing between the pillars was 'continually performed'.

In the natural course of things the public executions were a tourist attraction in themselves. From this point of view, few visitors can have had a more satisfactory introduction to the city than William Lithgow, who arrived in 1609. Originally from Lanark and known in his youth as 'cut-lugg'd Willie' after his ears had been cropped by the brothers of an early mistress, Lithgow spent much of his life in travels that were made even more perilous than necessary by his feverish anti-papism. This incident in Venice seems to be one of very few episodes that did something to stir his rather grim sense of humour:

> Mine Associate and I were no sooner landed, and perceiving a great throng of people, and in the midst of them a great smoak; but we began to demand of a *Venetian* what

the matter was? who replied there was a gray Friar burning quick at S. *Mark's* Pillar, of the reformed order of St. *Francis*, for begetting fifteen young noble Nunns with Child, and all within one year; he being also their Father Confessor. Whereat I sprung forward through the throng, and my Friend followed me, and came just to the Pillar as the half of his Body and right Arm fell flatlings in the fire: The Friar was forty six years old, and had been Confessor of that Nunnery of *Sancta Lucia* five years: Most of these young Nuns were Senators Daughters; and two of them were only come in to learn vertue, and yet fell in the midst of vice.

These fifteen with Child were all re-called home to their Fathers Palaces; the Lady Prioress, and the rest of her voluptuous Crew, were banished for ever from the Precincts of *Venice*. The Monastery was razed to the ground, their Rents were allowed to be bestowed upon poor Families, and distressed Age, and their Church to be converted to an Hospital.[19]

Unfortunately, as Lithgow explains, he and his companion had had nothing to eat, and 'being inhungred, and also overjoyed' by all this, they stumbled into an extravagantly expensive inn without checking the prices. Next morning the reckoning came:

> Mr *Arthur* look'd upon me, and I laugh'd upon him: In a word, our dinner and supper cost us forty Julets, twenty shillings *English*, being four Crowns, whereat my Companion being discontented, bad the Devil be in the Friars Ballocks, for we had paid soundly for his Leachery.[20]

THE DOGE'S PALACE

Lithgow's friar, like others who went the same way, had the doubtful consolation of breathing his last within sight of one of the most extraordinary buildings in the world. Extraordinary, at least, to modern eyes, but not to the average eighteenth-century traveller. 'There are but two squares in

Venice worth notice,' writes Major Ayscough robustly in his
Letters from an Officer in the Guards, 'and they are the great and
little square of Saint Mark . . . The little one fronts the great
canal, and has in it part of the Doge's palace, which is a large
old pile, gloomy, and not very beautiful.'[21]

Other verdicts have been more generous. For Henry James
the whole experience is permeated by images of light. Every
sentence offers a variation on the same theme:

> This deeply original building is of course the loveliest
> thing in Venice, and a morning's stroll there is a wonder-
> ful illumination. Cunningly select your hour – half the
> enjoyment of Venice is a question of dodging – and enter
> at about one o'clock, when the tourists have flocked off to
> lunch and the echoes of the charming chambers have gone
> to sleep among the sunbeams. There is no brighter place
> in Venice – by which I mean that on the whole there is
> none half so bright. The reflected sunshine plays up
> through the great windows from the glittering lagoon
> and shimmers and twinkles over gilded walls and ceil-
> ings. All the history of Venice, all its splendid stately past,
> glows around you in a strong sea-light.[22]

By the measured standards of James's prose this sounds
almost frolicsome. Only an optimist would today imagine
that fellow-tourists were so easy to avoid. The long march
through the rooms of the Ducal Palace is not for the faint-
hearted: in summer the crowds, in winter a succession of
rooms that have been shut up or cordoned off. The effort is
worth making, but perhaps tomorrow.[23]

The Bridge of Sighs

Byron's line in *Childe Harold*, 'I stood in Venice, on the
"Bridge of Sighs"', reads strangely when one sees that the
bridge is in fact a covered passageway leading across the Rio di
Palazzo to the prisons. It was Byron, nonetheless, who did
most to invest it with the romantic appeal it still enjoys. He
was perhaps helped in this by William Beckford who had

passed across the bridge a couple of decades earlier, in the final years of the Republic. It was the sort of experience precisely calculated to appeal to Beckford's Gothic romanticism. In this account his imagination has already been overheated by a visit to the old prisons under the Leads:

> Abandoning therefore the sad tenants of the Piombi to their fate, I left the courts, and stepping into my bark, was rowed down a canal over which the lofty vaults of the palace cast a tremendous shade. Beneath these fatal waters the dungeons I have also been speaking of are situated. There the wretches lie marking the sound of the oars, and counting the free passage of every gondola. Above, a marble bridge, of bold majestic architecture, joins the highest part of the prisons to the secret galleries of the palace; from whence criminals are conducted over the arch to a cruel and mysterious death. I shuddered whilst passing below; and believe it is not without cause, this structure is named PONTE DEI SOSPIRI.[24]

This was too much of a good thing to last. In the next century W. D. Howells dismissed the bridge as a 'pathetic swindle' – a rough equivalent of Ruskin's uncompromising note in the *Venetian Index*:

> The well-known 'Bridge of Sighs', a work of no merit, and of a late period . . . owing the interest it possesses chiefly to its pretty name, and to the ignorant senti-mentalism of Byron.[25]

THE PIOMBI

The prisons have fared rather better than the bridge. No one since has quite matched Coryate's relish for them – 'a very fair prison, the fairest absolutely that ever I saw . . . I thinke there is not a fairer prison in all Christendome' – but they remained a focus of romantic attention throughout the nineteenth century. Although the *piombi* have now been demolished, they retain their hold on the imagination largely through their link with Casanova. They seem in reality to have been a good deal less terrible than popular tradition suggests. According to Casanova himself,

> What are called 'the leads' are not gaols but small furnished lock-ups, with barred windows, at the top of the ducal palace, and the inmate is said to be 'under the leads' because the roof is covered with sheets of lead over the larch-wood beams. These leaden sheets make the rooms cold in winter and very hot in summertime. But the air is good, you get enough to eat, a decent bed and everything else you need, clothes, and clean laundry when you want it. The Doge's servants look after the rooms and a doctor, a surgeon, an apothecary and a confessor are always on hand.[26]

As Balzac put it, 'there are ten thousand zinc-covered garrets in Paris which are worse, and people pay up to two hundred francs a year for them – men of talent, as well.'[27] But realities of this kind make little headway against myth. A recent airline magazine was still declaring that Casanova 'was locked up in the dark and dismal prison beside the Doge's Palace', and assuring its readers that they could 'visit the very same dungeons today'.

Perhaps it is pedantic to trouble about these things. Casanova would have been the first to agree that the *piombi* were not the place for a protracted stay. He had gone home one morning in the early hours to find that his casino had been ransacked by officers of the State Inquisitors on the pretext of looking for contraband salt. Signor Bragadin, his friend and patron, urged him to post to Florence and stay there till the danger had passed. Casanova rejected the advice and went back to his home, where at dawn on 26 July 1755 he was arrested. The same day he crossed the Bridge of Sighs and spent the next fifteen months under the Leads. (He was in fact condemned on 12 September to five years' imprisonment for atheism, but he himself was unaware of this.)

In arresting Casanova, the Inquisitors had acted with their usual speed; the report on him furnished by their pious spy, Giovanni Battista Manuzzi, is dated 17 July. It gives an interesting glimpse of his daily life: dinner at the houses of the nobility, relaxation at a wine-shop in the Frezzeria, business at the gaming-houses where he casually hazards vast sums of money, pleasure in the company of women of whatever rank or condition Venice has to offer. All too much for a Christian spy: 'Conversing with and becoming intimate with the said Casanova, one sees truly united in him misbelief, imposture, lasciviousness and voluptuousness in a manner to inspire horror.'[28]

On the night of 31 October 1756 Casanova, in company with a timorous monk who was also trying to escape, first got on to the roof by forcing a hole through the Leads and from there managed to break into another part of the Doge's Palace through a window overlooking the canal. After penetrating as far as possible, he found himself, scratched and bleeding, trapped in the hall next to the Sala delle Quattro Porte. Here he put on some decent clothes, which left him looking, he says, like a man of quality who had been beaten up in a brothel, and then sat down to wait for something to happen. Finally, he was noticed at the window by some idlers in the palace courtyard. They informed the watchman, who assumed that this must be someone he had inadvertently shut in the previous evening. When the door of the Hall was unlocked, Casanova strode past the startled man without a word, walked coolly down the Giants' Staircase, out through the Porta della Carta, across the Piazzetta, and into the first gondola he came to.

As the gondoliers struck out for Mestre, and the lights of the Giudecca fell away to the left, Casanova must have thought he was looking on the shadowy outlines of Venice for the last time. But changes in circumstance were the stuff of his life. In 1780 he was back again, acting as a spy for the Inquisitors, until a libel he published against a patrician forced him once more to flee the city, this time for good.

The Pozzi

The *pozzi*, or wells, were the palace dungeons, which can still be visited. Though a rather grimmer proposition than the

Leads, even they were probably a good deal above average for contemporary Europe. Not that this deterred later visitors from following Beckford's lead. Dickens went round the prisons in November 1844 and obviously made the most of the occasion:

> One cell I saw, in which no man remained for more than four-and-twenty hours; being marked for dead before he entered it. Hard by, another, and a dismal one, whereto, at midnight, the confessor came – a monk, brown-robed, and hooded – ghastly in the day, and free bright air, but in the midnight of that murky prison, Hope's extinguisher, and Murder's herald. I had my foot upon the spot, where, at the same dread hour, the shriven prisoner was strangled; and struck my hand upon the guilty door – low browed and stealthy – through which the lumpish sack was carried out into a boat, and rowed away, and drowned where it was death to cast a net.[29]

A quarter of a century later Mark Twain was still getting some mileage out of the instruments of torture shown to tourists, among them

> a devilish contrivance of steel, which enclosed a prisoner's head like a shell, and crushed it slowly by means of a screw. It bore the stains of blood that had trickled through its joints long ago, and on one side it had a projection whereon the torturer rested his elbow comfortably and bent down his ear to catch the moanings of the sufferer perishing within.[30]

No doubt there is a residue of truth behind these frightening tales. The scars and scratchings on the walls were not all put there by holiday-makers and Romantic poets – though in 1833 Bulwer Lytton's wife wrote home that 'the guide told us they were nearly effaced till Lord Byron had spent two days re-cutting them into the walls.'[31] Perhaps Byron was right. It would have been a pity to lose them. Even refurbished, they carry forward a tenuous memory of the hands that originally carved them. Molmenti tells us that in the Torreselle, above

the name *Luchinus de Cremona 1458 31 Jan.*, were scratched
merely the words '*Disce pati*' ('Learn to endure').

BROGLIO

The strange and grand exterior of the palace, begun in the
fourteenth century and partially reconstructed in the fifteenth
and sixteenth in the wake of a couple of devastating fires, has
been described in too many guide-books to warrant attention
here. For a brief and knowledgeable account the reader can do
no better than turn to J. G. Links's *Venice for Pleasure*.

Looking up at the lovely capitals today, we might sometimes get nudged aside by an impatient photographer, but on
the whole we have a pleasant time of it compared with our
eighteenth-century ancestor. The area round the Ducal Palace,
known formerly as the *broglio* or meadow, was a public
meeting-place, but also, it seems, an unofficial public lava-
tory. Alfonso Lowe quotes the remarks of an eighteenth-
century traveller on the 'nasty fellows' who 'let down their
breeches wherever and before whomsoever they please, so
that many open parts, including the Piazza and outside the
ducal palace, are dedicated to *Cloacina*, and you may see the
votaries at their devotions every hour of the day.'[32]

At about the same time Hester Piozzi, who during her first
marriage, as Mrs Thrale, had been the friend of Dr Johnson,
also found her enjoyment of the palace seriously over-
shadowed by the state of its surroundings:

> The truth is, our dear Venetians are nothing less than
> cleanly. St Mark's Place is all covered over in a morning
> with chicken-coops, which stink one to death, as nobody,
> I believe, thinks of changing their baskets; and all about
> the ducal palace is made so very offensive by the resort of
> human creatures for every purpose most unworthy of so
> charming a place, that all enjoyment of its beauties is
> rendered difficult to a person of any delicacy, and
> poisoned so provokingly, that I do never cease to wonder
> that so little police and proper regulation are established in

a city so particularly lovely to render her sweet and wholesome.[33]

The sensitive Beckford was accustomed to escape from the 'noxious atmosphere' of St Mark's by running up the campanile to 'breathe the fresh gales which blow from the Adriatic'.

To judge from Ruskin's comments in this letter to his father, any improvement by the middle of the nineteenth century had been strictly partial. Set beside that of Mrs Piozzi, his reaction offers a compact image of how closely the aesthetic had become linked to the moral in Victorian England:

> It is of no use, as far as I see – trying to protestantize these Italians. They are totally incapable of understanding the beauty of Christ's own character. The first thing to be done is to teach them common Decency – Manliness and Truth. They are at present a curious Hybrid between the Fox and the Pig. I may give you one most striking instance of their character – though it is one you cannot well read out to my mother. The four last arches of the Ducal palace next the bridge of sighs having been partially filled up in the Renaissance times, afford a series of corners which – ever since I have known Venice – have been used by the Italians as those portions of our railroad stations are which are externally described as being set apart for 'Gentlemen.' It is nearly impossible to approach the capitals, though among the most beautiful of the series; and this is on the broad front of the Palace – and in the place where the Venetian senators used to have their own separate walk – the most honourable and restricted piece of ground in Venice.[34]

Ruskin may have been overstating the former purity of the spot. When Gilbert Burnet came here in the 1680s, he found the gilded youth of Venice strolling to and fro under the arcade, taking the air as though it were the finest in the world, but 'honourable' is not a word that suggests itself to him:

> It seemed to me a strange thing to see the Broglio so full of graceful young Senators and Nobles, when there was so glorious a War on foot with the *Turks*, but instead of

being heated in Point of Honour to hazard their Lives, they rather think it an extravagant piece of folly for them to go and hazard it when a little Money can hire strangers that do it on such easie terms, and thus their Arms are in the hands of strangers, while they stay at home managing their intrigues in the Broglio, and dissolving their spirits among their Courtisans.[35]

Burnet clearly found this lack of enthusiasm for being killed by the Turks hard to fathom. One can only speculate what his response would be to the sellers of T-shirts, trinkets, and guide-books who have replaced the young nobles and their imbroglios.

EASTERN VENICE

Suggested route

Canals

500 metres

500 yards

250

250

0

0

Cpo. di S. Pietro

Canale di S. Pietro

Rio di S. Anna

Fondamenta Sant'Anna

Giardini Garibaldi

Giardini Pubblici

ARSENAL

Campo dell'Arsenale

Via Garibaldi

Campo della Celestia

Campo San Francesco della Vigna

Campo S. Trinità

Sottoportico dell'Angelo

Campo dell'Angelo

Campo dei Due Pozzi

Fondamenta dell'Arsenale

S. Giovanni in Bragora

Riva della Ca' di Dio

Military bakeries

Naval Museum

San Biagio

Campo S. Lorenzo

Campo Bandiera e Moro

Calle dei Preti

C. della Pietà

Santa Maria della Pietà

Calle Larga S. Lorenzo

Calle Cappello

Barbaria delle Tole

Scuola di San Giorgio degli Schiavoni

Riva degli Schiavoni

Sottoportico San Zaccaria

Corte Coppo

Campo S. Zaccaria

Riva

Sottoportico della Paglia

Ponte della Paglia

Bridge of Sighs

S. Lorenzo

Fondamenta di S. Giorgio d. Schiavoni

Fondamenta dei Furlani

Salizzada dei Greci

San Giorgio dei Greci

Sant' Antonin

Piazza S. Marco

Fnda. di San Lorenzo

5

EASTERN VENICE

Ponte della Paglia—Hotel Danieli—San Zaccaria—Riva degli Schiavoni—Santa Maria della Pietà—San Giorgio dei Greci and San Antonin—San Giorgio degli Schiavoni—San Lorenzo—Palazzo Dolfin—San Francesco della Vigna—Calli and Campi—Calle Magno—Arsenal—Castello—Public Gardens

PONTE DELLA PAGLIA

The Ponte della Paglia can usually be identified by the press of holiday-makers taking pictures of the Bridge of Sighs. Earlier tourists had the more arduous alternative of the sketch-book. In 1828 the American poet Longfellow, author of 'Hiawatha', was sketching here 'when a wench of a chambermaid emptied a pitcher of water from a window of the palace directly upon my head. I came very near slipping into the canal.'[1] Since this was in the middle of December, the experience must have been memorably uncomfortable.

Casanova had no cause to look with any fondness at the Bridge of Sighs, but the Ponte della Paglia makes a less sombre appearance in his memoirs. One afternoon, as he returned from Padua along the road which runs beside the Brenta, he had witnessed the upset of a coach containing a pretty woman and an officer in German uniform. The accident had lifted the woman's skirts and very nearly tipped her into the river. Only Casanova's prompt action had saved her from this last indignity. The next day he is back in Venice. It happens to be Ascension Day, when the Doge celebrates Venice's annual wedding with the sea. There is nothing exceptional about the episode, but it offers an attractive vignette of the endless party that seems to have been Venetian life in the eighteenth century. (Anyone who has visited the Ca' Rezzonico and seen Pietro Longhi's picture of the rhinoceros on public display will have no difficulty in imagining the scene advertised by the poster at which Casanova's masked seductress is looking):

I was drinking coffee unmasked under the Procuratie in the Piazza San Marco when a beautiful female masker who was passing by gave me a playful blow on the shoulder with her fan. Not knowing the masker, I pay no attention. After drinking my coffee I put on my mask and make my way to the Riva del Sepolcro, where Signor Bragadin's gondola was waiting for me. Near the Ponte della Paglia I see the same masker who had struck me with her fan staring at the picture of a caged monster which was shown to anyone curious enough to give ten soldi to go in. I approach the masked lady and ask her what right she had had to strike me.

'To punish you for not recognizing me after you saved my life yesterday beside the Brenta.'

I compliment her, I ask her if she intends to follow the Bucentaur, and she answers that she would go if she had a perfectly safe gondola; I offer her mine, which is of the largest; she consults with the officer whom, though he is masked, I recognize by his uniform, and she accepts. . . . We followed the Bucentaur. As I am sitting on the bench beside the lady, I take a few liberties under cover of her cloak; but she discourages me by changing her position. After the ceremony we return to Venice, we disembark at the Colonne, and the officer says that they would be happy if I would dine with them at the 'Wild Man'. I accept. I had become greatly interested in the woman, who was pretty and of whom I had seen something more than her face. The officer left me alone with her, going on to order dinner for three.

I at once told her that I loved her, that I had a box at the opera, that I offered it to her, and that I would attend her throughout the fair if she would assure me that my time should not be lost.[2]

So they head for the Wild Man, an inn whose name is still borne by the Calle Selvadego just off the Piazza, and the whole process of seduction and intrigue is set in motion once again.

In earlier times Casanova's purposes could have been served nearer to hand. At the Ponte della Paglia in the fourteenth century there was an inn called The Dragon, which was kept by an Englishman. It was here that in March 1365, while Sir Henry Stromin was waiting in Venice to make the spring voyage to the Holy Land, two of his grooms, whose names are given in the State papers as John and Robin, became embroiled with a local artisan. George Parks summarizes the details to be found in the city's archives:

It seems that a Venetian named Mioranza, a cap-maker, made use of the inn to urinate in the straw behind one of the Englishman's horses. The two grooms rushed him out; he returned with a stone which he had picked up, threw it at Robin's head, but missed. John thereupon took him by the beard; he stabbed John with a bread knife, killing him, and ran away. Robin ran after him up the street inland; the fugitive jumped into the canal beyond the bridge to San Zaccaria, and was pulled into the basement windows of a house on the canal by two women who appeared there. The police at once made enquiry. Presumably justice was done, but we know no more of what may well have been a characteristic travel incident.[3]

Hotel Danieli

Ahead of us stretches the Riva degli Schiavoni. The second street on the left is the Calle delle Rasse, on the corner of which Doge Vitale Michiel II was murdered in 1172. Venice had a violent way with early Doges who failed to give satisfaction.

Vitale Michiel had just returned from an unlucky expedition to treat with the Emperor of Byzantium and was wisely removing himself from the attentions of the mob when he turned down the Calle delle Rasse. The assassin had anticipated him.

It was later discovered that the man had sheltered in one of the houses at the top of the calle, and these were accordingly razed to the ground. For almost eight centuries nothing was built there but the humble wooden structures we can see in paintings by Canaletto and others. Only in 1948 did the Hotel Danieli at last get permission to use the space for the construction of its new wing. The result does little credit to Venice's most distinguished hotel.

'The beginning of everything was in seeing the Gondola-beak come actually inside the door at Danieli's, when the tide was up, and the water two feet deep at the foot of the stairs.'[4] So Ruskin described in *Praeterita* the start of his obsession with Venice. Previously known as the Palazzo Dandolo, the Danieli had been partly converted to a hotel in 1822 by a Swiss, Joseph dal Niel,[5] and it was here that the newly married Ruskins stayed while John was writing the first volume of *The Stones of Venice*. On 13 November 1849 Effie writes to her mother: 'We are living in Danieli's Hotel, formerly a splendid Palace with marble staircase and doors and Balconies looking out on the sea covered with ships and churches and the Doge's Palace, the finest building in the world, with St Mark's Place & Church 100 yards off.'[6] Their first-floor sitting-room, no. 32 in the Danieli today, was in front, at the far end on the Piazzetta side.

Fifteen years earlier the hotel had witnessed the end of the tempestuous affair between George Sand and Alfred de Musset. The relationship was already precarious when they arrived, and de Musset's illness finished it off. While he sweated in the bedroom, Sand took stock of the young Dr Pagello who had been called in to treat him. Soon they were lovers – less spectacularly than Sand and de Musset, but perhaps more happily. Years afterwards Pagello described finding the feverish de Musset 'in a large room with windows overlooking the Riva degli Schiavoni, where there was a couch, a fireplace protected by a screen, a large table and, adjoining, a darkened room with two beds'.[7] Such was the setting for the violent, wearisome scenes that were to ensure Sand and de Mussett their place in the Pantheon of romantic lovers.

A later guest, in every way more discreet, was Marcel Proust: 'When I went to Venice I found that my dream had become – incredibly but quite simply – *my address*.'[8]

San Zaccaria

Fifty yards beyond the Danieli, a sottoportico leads down to the campo and church of San Zaccaria. Adjoining the campanile, behind a small garden, can be seen parts of the old Benedictine convent, patronized by the nobility and famed for its licentiousness. Max Beerbohm wrote evocatively of the campo as it appeared to him in the early years of the century:

> Nowhere in Venice is a more Venetian thing than this little, melancholy shabby Campo; this work of so many periods; this garment woven by so many cunning weavers, and worn threadbare, and patched and patched again, and at length discarded. Few people, and they poorest among the poor, live here now. One can hardly imagine that the well-head was ever open, ever gossiped around. Shutters interpolated in delicate Gothic windows are mouldering on their hinges; shutters that seem hardly incongruous now that they have been blistered by so many summers, and are so faded and so crazy. Piteous is the expression of gaunt misery on the façade of the church. The old low building that straggles away from beneath the tower and is railed off from the pavement, was once a nunnery, the richest of all the nunneries in Venice. A sentinel stands at its door; and now and again a soldier passes in or out, looking depressed. No children play here. A cat or two may be seen lying about when the sun shines. And the brightlier shines the sun the sadder seems the Campo San Zaccaria, seeming, indeed, to shrink away from the sun's rays, like a woman who has been beautiful, or like a woman who is ill.[9]

Today this seems rather harsh. The campo is often empty, and a little bare after the activity of the Riva, but it is a

respectable spot, well-kept even, compared with much of
Venice. In the middle is the well-head which figures in the
pretty legend Beerbohm tells about the square:

> And it was here, . . . on Michaelmas morning, that a
> devil, in the guise of a very beautiful youth, came and,
> smiling, plucked by the sleeve the bride of Sebastiano
> Morosini, and whispered in such sweet wise that she let
> go the arm of her bridegroom and gave her hand to the
> stranger. Sebastiano would have drawn his sword, but,
> under a spell that the devil had cast, it stayed in its
> scabbard. By a frantic inspiration of the moment, he went
> down on his hands and knees, and, crawling, roared,
> insomuch that the devil (having, like all the devils of that
> day, a share of simplicity) mistook him for the lion of S.
> Mark, and instantly vanished. Nor, so far as we know,
> did he ever reappear. But Sebastiano's stratagem, S.
> Mark's miracle, had laid such hold on the hearts of the
> Venetians that every man who was soon to be married
> would come on Michaelmas morning to the Campo San
> Zaccaria, and crawl once around the well-head, roaring.
> Thereby, it was thought, he assured for himself happiness
> of wedlock: his wife would never be inconstant to him,
> even in thought. She, the intended wife, accompanied
> him, with her parents, and with his parents, to see the
> pious little ceremony performed. All through Michael-
> mas morning the Campo San Zaccaria was crowded.
> Carpaccio painted a picture of the scene: a scene after his
> own heart . . .[10]

Some four centuries later, on Michaelmas morning 1906,
Beerbohm posts himself in the shadow of the sottoportico and
waits. He is on the point of giving up when a small party of
peasants appears, dressed in their Sunday clothes:

> There were six of them – two middle-aged men, two
> middle-aged women, and a young man, and a girl. For a
> minute or so they stood talking. Then the young man
> detached himself from the group, tossing his sombrero to
> an elder, and came across to the well-head. There, having

crossed himself, he went down on his hands and knees, and did as Sebastiano had done before him; and, little though the roaring may have been like a lion's, I did not once smile on my way home along the Riva Schiavoni.[11]

The Carpaccio painting was stolen from the church and lost for ever, but Giovanni Bellini's *Madonna and Saints* has had better luck. In 1845 Ruskin wrote to his father, 'There is a glorious John Bellini which the priests are burning to pieces with their candles.'[12] He had thoughts at the time of getting it back to England, but in San Zaccaria it has stayed, in the middle of the left aisle, looking better now after its restoration than it has done, perhaps, for most of its life.

At the far end of the square, beside the street leading towards the Campo San Provolo, is a tablet threatening the usual 'severe penalties' for gambling, swearing, and general misbehaviour in the campo. Given the pace at which the nuns were living, a casual blasphemer might reasonably have felt hard done by when faced with the prospect of prison, cord,[13] and galleys.

RIVA DEGLI SCHIAVONI

Continuing along the Riva, we pass at no. 4161 the green shutters of what is now the Pensione Wildner. It was from the windows of this building that Henry James looked out across the lagoon while he worked on *The Portrait of a Lady*:

> I had rooms on Riva Schiavoni, at the top of a house near the passage leading off to San Zaccaria; the waterside life, the wondrous lagoon spread before me, and the ceaseless human chatter came in at my windows, to which I seem to myself to have been constantly driven, in the fruitless fidget of composition, as if to see whether, out in the blue channel, the ship of some right suggestion, of some better phrase, of the next happy twist of my subject, the next true touch for my canvas, mightn't come into sight. . . .
> There are pages of the book which, in the reading over,

have seemed to make me see again the bristling curve of
the wide Riva, the large colour-spots of the balconied
houses and the repeated undulation of the little hunch-
backed bridges, marked by the rise and drop again, with
the wave, of foreshortened clicking pedestrians. The
Venetian footfall and the Venetian cry – all talk there,
however uttered, having the pitch of a call across the
water – come in once more at the window, renewing
one's old impression of the delighted senses and the
divided, frustrated mind.[14]

A short way further along the Riva, close to the Ponte del
Sepolcro, a plaque between nos. 4144 and 4143 marks the site
of Petrarch's house. This was the Palazzo delle Due Torre,
whose twin towers can just be seen in the famous Bodleian
picture of the departure of Marco Polo. Petrarch came to
Venice in 1362, having arranged to bequeath his library to the
Republic in exchange for the use of this house. It was here in
the following spring that he entertained Boccaccio, and from
the upper windows of the palace that he looked out on the
cradle of Venice's maritime power.

In a letter which conveys something of the restless enter-
prise that inspired the city's commercial expansion through
the fourteenth century he describes the scene one squally
night, when the shouts of the sailors reach him through the
storm. Putting down his pen, he goes to the window and looks
out to sea at the ships which have been moored there for the
winter, their masts reaching above the towers of his house:

The larger of the two ships was at this moment – though
the stars were all hidden by the clouds, the winds shaking
the walls, and the roar of the sea filling the air – leaving the
quay and setting out upon its voyage. . . . If you had seen
it, you would have said it was no ship but a mountain
swimming upon the sea, although under the weight of its
immense wings a great part of it was hidden in the waves.
The end of the voyage was to be the Don, beyond which
nothing can navigate from our seas; but many of those
who were on board, when they had reached that point,
meant to prosecute their journey, never pausing till they

had reached the Ganges or the Caucusus, India and the Eastern Ocean.[15]

Santa Maria della Pietà

Between James's house and Petrarch's stands Santa Maria della Pietà, the church where Vivaldi was concert-master. It was originally attached to an orphanage, which had been moved here from San Francesco della Vigna in the early sixteenth century. If you walk down the Calle della Pietà, you can still see at the corner of the church a plaque, dated 12 November 1548, invoking God's anger against those who leave their children here without need. The macabre background to this hospital is explained by Pero Tafur, a well-to-do Spaniard who had visited Venice in 1436 as part of his European tour:

> In times past there were few weeks, or even days, when the fishermen did not take out dead babies from their nets, and this, they say, came from the fact that the merchants were so long separated from their wives. These, urged by their fleshly lusts, gave way to them and became pregnant, and with intent to save their reputations threw the offspring out of the window into the sea as soon as they were delivered, the place being aptly disposed therefor. The rulers, in view of such enormous crimes, took counsel together and founded a great and rich hospital, very finely built, and placed in it a hundred wet-nurses to suckle the babes, and now those who would hide their shame take their children there to be reared.[16]

Tafur goes on to mention a further humane provision, which has a pleasantly Venetian twist. The papal bull secured by the city granted various pardons to anyone who visited the children in hospital. Without giving themselves away, the parents could thus go to see their children under colour of religious exercise.

To the outsider charitable bequests often seem a trifle eccentric, but few can have been more so than that received by the Pietà in 1697. An austere member of the Erizzo family had been so disgusted by contemporary fashions in dress that he left a special clause in his will disinheriting in favour of the Pietà any of his sons who had worn a periwig or red socks. This fell heavily on his son Niccolò whose addiction to the periwig was what had excited the old man's rage. In the event, Niccolò contested the will and managed to reach a compromise by which he handed over six thousand ducats but kept his wig and the rest of his fortune.

SAN GIORGIO DEI GRECI AND SAN ANTONIN

At the bottom of the Calle della Pietà a left turn quickly followed by a right will bring us into the street that leads past the back of San Giorgio dei Greci. (To get round to the front, turn left when you reach the Salizzada dei Greci.) This sixteenth-century Greek Orthodox church with its dangerous-looking campanile is not always easy to get into. The visitor must either beg admission from the custodian of the neighbouring museum or lie in wait for one of the unpredictable periods when the door is open.

Coryate had no such problems, happening upon the place during the morning service. He thought it 'a very faire little Church', but took exception to the congregation's practice of wagging their hands up and down. Their appearance, too, caused him some misgiving – 'Most of these Grecians are very blacke, and all of them both men and children doe weare long haire, much longer than any other mans besides that I could perceive in all Venice, a fashion unseemly and very ruffian-like.'[17]

It was only a few months before his death that Richard Wagner visited the church, on 11 October 1882. The markedly eastern flavour of the Greci seems to have disconcerted him; he was uneasy about it at the time and returned to the subject on the following day, as Cosima records in her diary: 'In the morning R. talks to me again about the Greci church, saying that it does not give any warm feelings of Christianity but, rather, an impression of stiffness and pomp, like a relic of ancient Assyria!'[18]

San Giorgio dei Greci today is still an oddity. The central cross is set in a screen of icons and the seats are ranged lengthwise along either side of the nave. Overhead, the dark cupola offers only the dim glow of the haloes of the saints depicted in its roof. Both style and atmosphere mark its difference from other Venetian churches.

The network of streets in this part of Venice is more than usually labyrinthine. It is an area into which tourists tend to stray only when they have lost their way to San Giorgio degli Schiavoni, so that chance rather than design takes most people to the church of San Antonin at the far end of the Salizzada dei Greci. Closed at the moment for restoration, it was once, according to W. D. Howells, a source of some displeasure to the local population. The trouble sprang from St Anthony's traditional association with the emblem of the pig:

> Among other privileges of the Church, abolished in Venice long ago, was that ancient right of the monks of S. Anthony, Abbot, by which their herds of swine were made free of the whole city. These animals, enveloped in an odour of sanctity, wandered here and there, and were piously fed by devout people, until the year 1409, when, being found dangerous to children and inconvenient to everybody, they were made the subject of a special decree, which deprived them of their freedom of movement.[19]

More recently, the church enjoyed brief notoriety in 1819 when a large male elephant took refuge there after escaping from its cage on the Riva degli Schiavoni. Small arms were used without effect on the maddened beast. After a period of chaos artillery was brought up and in the end the runaway elephant was, as Captain Douglas puts it rather unfeelingly, 'despatched by a shot from a piece of ordnance'. The episode left its mark on literature in the form of a pamphlet entitled *The Elephanticide in Venice in the year 1819 written by the noble signor Pietro Bonmartini of Padua* and a poem, recently reprinted, called 'Elefanteide'.

San Giorgio degli Schiavoni

In spite of various arrows that claim to show one the way, San Giorgio degli Schiavoni can be difficult to find. Fortunately, San Antonin is the easiest direction from which to approach it. On the right, as we walk down the Fondamenta dei Furlani, a calle leads into the little Corte Coppo, which was the home of the first woman to be quartered in Venice by way of punishment. Marin Sanudo records that on 1 May 1521, after twenty-two years of marriage, a certain Bernardina battered her husband to death, forced her daughter and a cousin to bury him and then gave out that he had gone on a pilgrimage to Loreto. It was only when a relative made enquiries in Loreto and Bernardina herself tried to interest a house-guest in digging up the ex-husband and reburying him more securely that the crime came to light.

What brings people here now is the marvellous group of paintings which line the ground-floor walls of the Scuola di San Giorgio degli Schiavoni. They are the work of Vittore Carpaccio, a painter whose most outlandish subjects are stamped with something quintessentially Venetian. Whatever their ostensible setting, the gorgeous architecture of Venice will usually find its way into the background. Equally constant, and perhaps equally Venetian, is an element of time-worn melancholy in the pictures; Carpaccio's characters have a languid elegance that makes them seem half-disengaged from the scene of which they are a part. Always his processions and regattas and receptions are witnessed by at least one youthful figure whose thoughts are caught in a dream. Not everyone feels quite the enthusiasm they express for Tintoretto, but it would be a strange and unsatisfactory person who could not love Carpaccio.

The room itself is not immediately prepossessing. It is, says Ruskin, 'a little room about the size of the commercial parlour of an old-fashioned English inn; perhaps an inch or two higher in the ceiling. . . .'[20] For Henry James the setting is still less acceptable, but as he looks at the painting of St Augustine in his study, he finds that even the sharpest criticism loses its edge:

It unites the most masterly finish with a kind of universal largeness of feeling, and he who has it well in his memory will never hear the name of Carpaccio without a throb of almost personal affection. Such indeed is the feeling that descends upon you in that wonderful little chapel of St George of the Slaves, where this most personal and sociable of artists has expressed all the sweetness of his imagination. The place is small and incommodious, the pictures are out of sight and ill-lighted, the custodian is rapacious, the visitors are mutually intolerable, but the shabby little chapel is a palace of art.[21]

In most respects things have improved since James's time; one's fellow-visitors may still be intolerable, but the lighting now is good, the charges are fixed, and, if you pick your time, you can gaze at leisure from the relative comfort of a bench.

In Ruskin's view there is one particular detail that should claim our attention. Writing, still hypnotically, in wayward and obsessed old age, he directs us to the painting of the *Triumph of St George*. We should for the moment disregard the figures of St George himself and the conquered dragon and instead focus our opera glass on the heads of the two princely riders to the left – the Saracen king and his daughter – he in high white turban, she beyond him in the crimson cap, high, like a castle tower:

Look well and long. For truly, – and with hard-earned and secure knowledge of such matters, I tell you, through all this round world of ours, searching what the best life of it has done of brightest in all its times and years, – you shall not find another piece quite the like of that little piece of work, for supreme, serene, unassuming, unfaltering sweetness of painter's perfect art. Over every other precious thing, of such things known to me, it rises, in the compass of its simplicity; in being able to gather the perfections of the joy of extreme childhood, and the joy of a hermit's age, with the strength and sunshine of mid-life, all in one.

Which is indeed more or less true of all Carpaccio's

work and mind; but in this piece you have it set in close
jewellery, radiant, inestimable.[22]

SAN LORENZO

The bridge in front of the Scuola leads across to the Fondamenta di San Giorgio degli Schiavoni. A short way down
this a calle to the left takes us round to the church of San
Lorenzo, set in a plain and peaceful campo with five trees and
five benches. Today the church, closed for restoration, presents a façade of crazed brick ridges which in its decrepitude
can look oddly appealing. It was here, four and a half centuries
ago, that Marco Polo was buried.

In a city notorious for the laxity of its convents, San Lorenzo
already enjoyed a reputation more colourful than most. Since
upper-class women were frequently dispatched to a convent
for financial reasons rather than to answer any vocation, it is
unsurprising that chastity to many seemed tiresome. It was
often the case that younger sons who might have made
husbands for them were being firmly directed to the brothel
rather than the marriage bed, in order to avoid any dispersal of
the family's estate. As the sixteenth-century scholar Roger
Ascham noted in *The Scholemaster*: 'I learned, when I was at
Venice that there it is counted good pollicie, when there be
foure or five brethren of one familie, one onelie to marie: and
all the rest to waulter with as little shame in open lecherie, as
Swyne do here in the common myre.'[23] The result was
inevitable. By the fourteenth century the Council had already
started passing laws to discourage the fornications of libertine
nuns and their partners, pleasantly called *monachini*. Convent
chaplains had to be fifty years old or more, while confessors,
by a nice distinction, had to be at least sixty.

The effects of these measures seem to have been disappointing. For successive centuries Venetian convents remained a
byword for dissolute living. To get some idea of their atmosphere, we need only look at Francesco Guardi's painting in the
Ca' Rezzonico of a convent *parlatorio*. It catches precisely the

tone that delighted Charles de Brosses when he visited the city in the eighteenth century. Having briefly described the squabble that was going on between three convents as to which should provide a mistress for the Papal nuncio who was soon to arrive, he adds:

> In truth, it would be to the nuns that I should most readily turn if I had to make a long stay here. All those I have seen through the grate at mass, chatting and laughing together as long as the service lasted, have struck me as good-looking and habited in such a way as to highlight their beauty. They have a charming little *coiffure* and a simple dress, but one that is of course perfectly white, revealing their shoulders and breasts to just the same degree as the dresses in the Roman style worn by our actresses.[24]

Across something over four centuries the convent of San Lorenzo recurs in the Venetian archives in one disreputable context after another. Its most famous graduate was probably Maria Da Riva, a patrician nun whose passionate affair with the French ambassador, Froulay, caused a diplomatic incident. Disguised only by a mask, Maria would leave San Lorenzo at night, accompany Froulay to the casinos, and then return to her convent with the dawn. When the State Inquisitors took exception to this and forbade her to meet the ambassador, Froulay ignored the prohibition and indignantly complained to Paris about his treatment. In the end, it was only by transferring Maria from San Lorenzo to a convent in Ferrara that the Inquisitors managed to resolve the situation – temporarily. Before long the incorrigible nun fell in love with an Italian colonel, fled to Bologna, and there got married.

In spite of everything, there was one event in its history which San Lorenzo could look back on with some complacency.

The summer of 1360 had not been a happy time for the convent. In June three men were imprisoned and fined for sleeping with some of the nuns, and then a month later another group of nuns was caught receiving love letters smuggled in by five women who were publicly whipped. It is a measure of divine tolerance that in the same year one of Venice's most celebrated miracles should have been staged on the convent's doorstep.

If you stand on the bridge at the far end of the campo, you will still be able to recognize enough of the surrounding architecture to identify the site of the *Miracle of the Holy Cross* from Gentile Bellini's painting in the Accademia. (In particular, the tall building which rises behind the house at the end of the fondamenta is unmistakable.) The Cross in question had fallen into the canal and then miraculously floated to the surface again so that it could be recovered. Bellini depicts the episode at the moment when a swimming prelate triumphantly holds up the Cross to the watching crowds on the Fondamenta di San Lorenzo.

To readers of the modern thriller the fondamenta will be familiar for other reasons, for it is here, just behind Bellini's line of spectators, that we find the entrance to police headquarters. Among the weary heroes and frightened villains who have passed this way, there are few who leave much impression on the mind. With its twisting alleys and sunless courtyards Venice seems to offer a perfect setting for the business of the crime-writer, but it has on the whole produced a disappointing crop.

PALAZZO DOLFIN

At the end of the fondamenta, a short way beyond the bridge, a left turn takes us into the Calle Larga San Lorenzo. Something less than a hundred yards down on the right a heavy door set into an archway gives access to the fifteenth-century Palazzo Dolfin at no. 5123. It was still relatively new when Pietro Casola saw it in 1494. The sixty-seven-year-old priest had just returned from a pilgrimage to the Holy Land and was preparing for the last stage of his journey back to Milan. His account of a visit to one of the Dolfin women who was in childbed gives a vivid image of the upper reaches of life in Venice at a time when England, less than ten years on from the Battle of Bosworth, was still hauling itself out of the Middle Ages:[25]